ROUTLEDGE LIBRARY EDITIONS: FOLKLORE

Volume 10

OLD WIVES' TALES

OLD WIVES' TALES
Life-Stories from Ibibioland

IRIS ANDRESKI

Routledge
Taylor & Francis Group

LONDON AND NEW YORK

First published in 1970

This edition first published in 2015
by Routledge
4 Park Square, Milton Park, Abingdon, Oxon OX14 4RN
605 Third Avenue, New York, NY 10017

Routledge is an imprint of the Taylor & Francis Group, an informa business

© 1970 Iris Andreski

British Library Cataloguing in Publication Data
A catalogue record for this book is available from the British Library

ISBN: 978-1-138-84217-5 (Set)
ISBN: 978-1-138-84353-0 (hbk)(Volume 10)
ISBN: 978-1-138-84557-2 (pbk)(Volume 10)

Publisher's Note
The publisher has gone to great lengths to ensure the quality of this reprint but points out that some imperfections in the original copies may be apparent.

Disclaimer
The publisher has made every effort to trace copyright holders and would welcome correspondence from those they have been unable to trace.

Iris Andreski

Old wives' tales

Life-Stories from Ibibioland

London   Routledge & Kegan Paul

First published 1970
by Routledge & Kegan Paul Limited
Broadway House, 68–74 Carter Lane
London, E.C.4
Printed in Great Britain by
Western Printing Services Ltd., Bristol
© *Iris Andreski 1970*
SBN 7100 6655 4

Mojemu kochanemu Stasiowi

'We regard the Ibibio people as the first ever made by God. Therefore they know more than other races of ancient knowledge concerning the making of the world, the coming of the first men and the secrets of the gods.'

Chief Amakiri Yellow,
(a chief of the Ijaw peoples of the Niger Delta)

As though it were their chosen
Way of being,
They lift necessity
And bear it on their heads.

From *African Women Walking*
by Barbara Noel Scott

Contents

Contents

Preface

This collection of Ibibio lives was begun in Eastern Nigeria, when I was assisting my husband in a survey of the effects of rapid urbanization upon the hitherto agricultural people of that area.* The Efik-Ibibio group is by reputation composed of the earliest settlers in the Niger Delta, and therefore the best choice of a link with the unrecorded past.

A second volume is in preparation in which the life-style of the modern urban Nigerian woman is contrasted with that of her recent ancestors, stressing the considerable alteration in the relationship between the sexes caused by her emancipation.

The more rural of these studies were made with the aid of several young Ibo, Ibibio and Ijaw ladies, whose detachment and integrity I cannot sufficiently praise, though the education of most of them was so fragmentary that they would otherwise have remained unemployed.

The work has been completed under the auspices of the Sociology Dept. of the University of Reading, helped by a grant from the University's Research Board, and also with the kind and invaluable assistance of Miss Barbara McCallum of the St Andrew's Mission, Diobu, who has co-ordinated my long-distance research. I am also deeply indebted to my husband for information concerning political institutions, and for the stern intellectual discipline which has kept me within the bounds of reason and factuality. I am grateful to Mrs Yates also, for patiently reading and typing this collection.

I have chosen to publish these stories in a form of English which is as near as possible to the vernacular in which they were told, while being intelligible to the ordinary English

* Owing to the Biafran war, all of this survey is no longer of relevance but the conclusions which apply to other parts of the continent have been treated in *The African Predicament, a study in the pathology of modernisation* by Stanislaw Andreski Michael Joseph, London, 1968 and Atherton Press, N.Y., 1969.

reader. In this I have been greatly helped by Miss Asari Edem, an Efik lady of beauty and distinction who is able to speak the kind of Nigerianized English (not to be confused with 'pidgin'), which has not been purged by foreign travel of the poetic speech-rhythms, proverbs and verbal mannerisms of the original tongues. The language spoken by Nigerians who have undergone a few years of primary schooling, though grammatically eccentric, has a daintiness and elegance infinitely to be preferred to the clumsy speech of contemporary Britain.

I have regretfully been forced to alter expressions using the double verb effects which have been demonstrated so skilfully by Gabriel Okara in his exquisite novel, *The Voice*. For example, the lady bewailing her seduction by a man from another tribe, says in the original statement:

'I only wait for the day he will marry his townsgirl come, there and then will I carry my child go', which has some of the lilting beauty of Okara's translations, but unfortunately would hold up most readers.

I have left many 'Nigerianisms' of speech which are to me more graceful than the modern Americanized English now coming into use in Nigerian schools. Some of these have their roots in the biblical language of the Missions, some in the Law Courts; but many are based on the striking speech-patterns of a people who had to say something memorable if it were to be remembered, since it could not be committed to paper.*

The reader must not be surprised to come across fragments of ethnological jargon in some otherwise naïve stories. The illiteracy of these women is that of circumstance, not of incompetence. A term like 'subsistence economy' picked up from a grandson's conversation, is perfectly comprehensible to an intelligent woman who has spent her life participating in such.

English literary critics who occasionally show incredulity at the elaborate complexity of the conversational language of peasants and market-women in novels by African writers are unfortunately demonstrating their ignorance. The verbal heritage of the African is so rich that education has brought about a kind of literary explosion. It would seem almost impossible for a West African of this

* An equally striking phenomenon is the oral literature of the pastoral peoples of the Horn of Africa, which has been collected and translated by B. W. Andrzejewski in *Somali Poetry*, Oxford, 1964.

generation to write a bad novel, and next decade may see a Biafran Tolstoy, or a Guinean Proust.

The collection in this book is however chiefly of value as a human document. Apart from the historical and anthropological content, these stories are, I believe, important in banishing the myth of primitivity, the 'heart of darkness' which is still the popular image of the African interior. The women who tell the stories though like any peasants, perplexed by superstitions and confined within rigid customs, emerge as psychologically 'modern'. Although their life-styles are, on the whole, those of their ancestors, there is no sign whatever of the unawakened savage in a condition of 'participation mystique' with nature or fellow-beings.

One may also remark that, in comparison with their menfolk, they seem singularly unruffled by the presence of the whiteman in their land, having had in contrast little to lose by change.

22 February 1968   I.A.

Introduction

It is not usual to regard old wives' tales as a reservoir of wisdom, but rather as an irrational heritage of superstition. One doubts their validity because they are based on unquestioning acceptance of questionable authority. As often as not, they represent a chain of unbroken loyalty to ancient principles whose logic is forgotten but whose power has accumulated through the continual reinforcement of early indoctrination. The emotional pressure contained in their often false cosmologies is of danger to the young, and has acquired a justly suspect reputation.

But the wisdom of old wives is not always an accumulation of fantasy; even though women who have been kept in a kind of protective custody, unable to acquire experience through trial and error, might well produce old wives' tales whose compounded distortion can contribute to the undermining of their civilization through the propagation of unreason to the most vulnerable.

The old Ibibio wives of this book have to a large extent escaped this social catastrophe. So much of their life is purely pragmatic, concerned with the immediate requirements of survival, that they appear as often as not more flexible of mind than their menfolk, and, segregated from a male culture of self-perpetuating obscurantism, more wholesomely reasonable.

Beyond this, a nobler ethic has been forced upon them almost by accident, through their deprivation of the fruits of cupidity. If they cherish their husbands, their motives are pure of material considerations since they themselves are the providers. If they love their sons, it is not because these will sacrifice their livestock to ensure their passage to heaven, as this function is reserved for their father. Neither does their love for their daughters hang upon expectations of bride-price, since most of this also will go to the father.

The Ibibio old wives (and the Ibo and the Yoruba) have perforce been spared some of the more stultifying effects of their husbands' complex rural culture. Many of these autobiographies demonstrate the natural growth of responsibility and dignity which has filled their cultural vacuum.

However, these stories are by no means moral tracts. My original intention in asking the oldest available women to give their life-histories was to obtain a first-hand record of a pattern of human life which the impact of a foreign civilization had nearly erased and which has been much less publicized than its masculine counterpart. As it happens, the collection is shorter than I could have wished since my work was terminated by the fratricidal struggle which still rends Nigeria at the time of writing, presumably marking the end of a long chapter of traditional African history.

The women who have written these lives, though elderly, are only to a small degree pre-colonial. They come from the area penetrated by the archetypal missionary, Mary Slessor, but it was with their mothers that she dealt. Nevertheless, although professing Christianity, most have lived according to the code of their grandmothers. For this reason, I cannot leave their stories to explain themselves but must first give some description of significant rituals and the daily routine which the Ibibio women share with those of most other West African coastal tribes. This will involve some History, but let me first dispose of Geography by saying that the Ibibios inhabit an area with one of the heaviest rainfalls in the African tropical rain-forest; that they practise agriculture in what is normally jungle; and that their children die of malaria almost as easily as the first European adventurers. The tsetse fly makes it impossible to rear cattle or horses, and the proliferation of the vegetation has until recently made wheeled vehicles impracticable.

It is quite impossible to appreciate the life-style of the traditional West African without some knowledge of the austere, low-yielding and laborious form of agriculture known as 'swidden farming'.

In tropical rain-forests, all over the world, agriculture has been until very recently frozen at the pioneering stage of clearing a plot, burning it, growing crops there for a while among the stumps and roots, then leaving it to revert to forest and moving on.

In more temperate zones, this is normally followed by a wave of more permanent settlement and improved methods of farming. Well-meaning agriculturalists who have attempted to transplant the high-yielding temperate systems to the tropics by large-scale forest clearance, deep ploughing and yearly sowing, have, after initial success, met with disaster in the form of leached soil, unusable land and eventual famine. They have been led to infer that the system of bush fallow rotation common to Melanesia, Uganda, the Congo etc, was based on native experience of crop success or failure over many centuries.

Actually, swidden farming, though it appears at first sight highly wasteful, is one of the few methods of conserving fertility in a tropical soil. The long fallow periods are essential for replacing organic matter to the heavily rain-washed earth, and the burning of the bush redresses the chemical balance of the soil.

Where population grows, land must eventually be used again, and thus rotation systems develop. In Ceylon, for example, one to three years of farming are followed by as many as twenty years fallow; in New Guinea, one year cropping requires fifteen years fallow.

In Ibibioland, it has been customary in most areas to farm for one year and leave six years fallow. (This is the method by which many of the old wives have calculated their age—thus allowing for an error of seven years in either direction.)

The plots of land, or 'bush' as they are described in the stories, have become the hereditary property of each extended family and are not considered saleable, although occasionally they may be rented. Quarrels between families or villages are usually over bordering plots. Quarrels between women also take place at the time of the year when their husband allot the family swiddens to his wives to farm, some being inevitably more fertile than others.

The work is divided up; older men do not take part in the labour, either from decrepitude, or because they have bought exemption through village 'titles'. Younger or poorer or hired men do the heavy felling, and women and boys the lighter trimming and spreading of debris which is then burned in the dry season. Sowing, weeding and harvesting is the women's work, unless they can afford to hire young men to help them. With the exception of the yam, the produce is considered the women's property, and they can market whatever is left over from feeding their families. Women often form small collectives with their personal friends, and hoe each other's lands in turn, either for safety or to keep each other company, singing together as they work. They do not grumble about this heavy labour in the sun-drenched and steaming fields;

indeed, their self-respect depends upon it, and one of the chief complaints of husbands is that ambitious wives neglect the home for the farm.

Unfortunately, petty squabbles over land-plots between wives or families are merely symptomatic of a generalized conflict which reflects a very serious state of affairs. It is quite clear that by the time the trading nations of Europe made their first serious penetrations of the West African interior, the utilization of the land by primitive shifting cultivation had reached saturation point. This is clearly shown by the fact that each agricultural village was by then an armed garrison and that women farmers whenever possible hired body-guards when walking any distance to their plots.

The principle of militarism following upon land saturation has been strikingly elucidated by Russell and Russell* with regard to the prehistoric Danubian farmers. But in the tropical rain-belt, land-starvation invariably leads to more drastic methods of population control such as were clearly observable in the West African rural communities at the time of the first missionary establishments. The most tragic evidence of a human ecological crisis were the centres for mass extermination at Benin and Aro-Chukwu, where human sacrifice had acquired the character and dimensions of a corrupt industry.

Many of the human beings who made the notorious 'Atlantic passage', owed their survival to the fact that the priesthood found an additional source of income in the preservation for sale of sacrificial victims, thus passing the problems of an expanding population to another generation in another continent.

However, the human-skull-studded trunks of trees of religious centres such as Aro demonstrate conclusively the demographic sur-plus which had already made itself felt before the intervention of foreign powers to aggravate the situation with enforced pacifism and hygiene.

The fratricidal struggles which rend the Asian and African nations evacuated by the European colonists are an horrific memorial to the vast hubris of those who believed that the precarious ethics of the affluent societies could be enforced upon the poor.

This was to some extent predicted by Mary Kingsley, the Cassan-dra of colonization, who foresaw that trade, minus Mission or Administration, was the only feasible approach of Britain to West

* *Violence, Monkeys and Men.*

Africa. For raising her voice on this subject she was quickly despatched to a plague-spot; human-sacrifice not being the monopoly of
tribal man.

The impact of the great Niger Delta on early expatriate travellers
varied considerably. Sir Richard Burton described it as a detestable
site for the erection of any town even at its best, where 'matted
masses of foetid verdure rise in terrible profusion around'. Mary
Kingsley, on the other hand, writes, 'the great swamp region of the
Bight of Biafra . . . in its immensity and gloom . . . has a grandeur
equal to that of the Himalayas', but she adds—typically—that it isn't
everybody's cup of tea.

Before my own visit to West Africa, I was told by a shining-eyed
student from Nigeria's Eastern Region (as it was then) that the
country around Port Harcourt resembled the Garden of Eden. But a
Yoruba lady who had been there added, drily, that 'there is very little
of God's handiwork in that area'.

Dr and Mrs Amaury Talbot, who spent many years in the Delta
around the second decade of this century, both in administrative and
anthropological work, have filled many volumes with what is
undoubtedly the most valuable research on the area and its people.
And although their writing is admirable in its scientific detachment,
it is quite obvious that they were bewitched by the place and its
inhabitants, and that Burton's black and muddy pools were for them
enchanted glades inhabited by naiads. Indeed, if the forests of West
Africa are truly peopled by ghosts, as local tradition insists, how
many wandering spirits of district officers there must be, and (dare I
say it?) part-paganized spirits of missionaries. For, regardless of its
often uncomfortable geography, Africa has the power of creating
expatriate patriots, the souls of whom one cannot imagine at rest
elsewhere.

Nevertheless, the hardship of life in mangrove swamp and tropical
rain-forest must not be underestimated, and it seems likely that so
inclement an environment could never have been regarded as a
promised land, a first choice for wandering nomads. On the contrary,
except for a few fishers and traders, about whom records exist from
classical times, the massive populations seem to have been pushed
south from the more fertile regions fringing the Sahara, in successive
waves over the centuries, by the organized and mounted forces
of semi-arab peoples and, later, during the great slaving century,
quite literally sold down the river to await purchase in the Delta.

Apparently the termination of the slave trade left this area with a greater proportion of slaves than freemen.

Such is the picture given by Talbot, but a possibly more enlightening account of the history of these peoples is found in Professor Onwuku Dike's scholarly and definitive work *Trade and Politics in the Niger Delta*, an important corrective to the romantic view of 'primitive' Africa. Professor Dike, in contrast to Talbot, believes that many of the coastal tribes came to the delta region by way of Benin (thus accounting for their culture and language, which is in many features sharply contrasting with that of the Ibos); and places their migrations as pre-fifteenth century, and thus before the advent of the Portuguese traders.

However, the small fishing and salt-making villages which resulted from these early migrations were enormously enhanced by the Atlantic trade, which drew down the peoples of the hinterland, and established such ports as Bonny, turning the Delta into the 'Venice of Africa'.

The Ibibio and Efik peoples are considered to have joined the Ijaws in the coastal trade during its heyday, though traditionally they place their origins in the Cameroons.

The merchant peoples of the coast can still be heard to comment on the social inferiority of the Ibos, many of whom are the descendants of slaves. Nevertheless, the ability of the latter to turn thraldom into princedom, as in the famous case of King Jaja, is a typical indication of the indomitable vitality and high intelligence of this group, which clearly shows itself through their present tragic circumstances.

Concerning the monstrous slave trade, so much has been written that I need say no more than that it was so recent and accepted an institution that many of the women who give their life stories in this book mention specifically that they were freeborn or, when otherwise, admit only to a noteworthy form of slave-birth, as in the case of the daughter of a favoured slave of a chief. Slavery is mentioned in these autobiographies in two other contexts: one is the expression of regret in the passing of slavery, since parents are now left with no effective threat with which to command the obedience of teenagers. The other is a reference to the predominantly Ibo, and still effective stigma of 'Osu' slave descent, that is, of being descended from a person who had been dedicated to the service of a local shrine and was therefore holy or untouchable. Such people may formerly have been sacrificed to a deity, but apparently the custom had lapsed and these slaves had become a caste of 'non-persons', ostracized and unmarriageable except to each other. Tradition has it that 'Osu' girls are singularly beautiful and desirable, but such qualities are usually associated with the forbidden. Shortly after Independence, the Nigerian government illegalized discrimination against such slave castes,* but this law is sadly confined to paper, as it takes more than one generation to wipe out a powerful tabu. Mr Chinua Achebe has written a tragic story of two educated and sensitive Nigerians whose love was unable to survive the consciousness of this stigma, and although the author could clearly see both sides of this tragedy, an African reviewer of his novel (*No Longer at Ease*) in *Drum Magazine*, envisaged the stigmatized girl as actually evil and menacing.

In one of the following Ibibio life-stories, a woman describes the break-up of her marriage on her discovery that her husband came from this despised caste, although she has no other complaint to make against him.

It seems likely, however, that a smaller proportion of the Ibibios were slaves than among the Ibo-speaking people; nor were so many of them slave-traders as were the Ijaw or 'Rivers' people. If they had a speciality, it seems to have been medicine. An abnormally high percentage of the accompanying stories are by wives or daughters of native doctors, who, we must remember, also function as psychologists, pharmacists and priests, though heads of families and village title-holders have often more important priestly status.

Native medicine is a hereditary profession and its secrets may die with a practitioner if he has no sons. It is not however entirely confined to men. A doctor's wife, for example, may have to collect his herbs, just as any other wife would be expected to farm a man's lands, and consequently, if left a widow, she may continue to practise as a herbalist.

In order to give you some impression of the type of medicine practised in Ibibio land, I shall include here a description of his methods by a traditional Ibibio doctor; he informs us:

There are so many methods of treating people. All depends on the type of sickness. I shall only describe one and that is 'witchcraft'. If a person is sick of witchcraft, I first of all climb on top of a cotton tree to go and do some sacrifice there so as to bring

* January, 1956.

back the voice of the patient which the witch has changed.
When this is done, the patient who remained dumb must talk
immediately, then I know that he will recover if I start to give
treatment. Second step is for me to take the ash of those expert
witches who died, mix with some herbs and give the patient to
drink for prevention against the devil coming in to worry. After,
the patient will start to recover, then I present the sacrifice in
the big forest at about 12.00 p.m. When the patient is well, this
is the time I bless the patient. The blessing is always done by
digging a grave in my backyard, lay the patient inside. If a man,
I tied one cock on his left foot, and if a woman I use a female
cock. I light seven candles on the head and seven on the foot.
Then I conjure all the powerful spirits who died to come and do
the rest of the job. The patient is to remain there for seven days,
eat there, do everything there till the seven days is completed
before I bring him out and shoot a gun before I bid him bye-bye.
That ends all about my treatment.

Methods of this kind may appear ludicrous, but an experienced
psychiatrist will appreciate their value. European-trained African
psychiatrists, after having introduced modern methods into Nigerian
hospitals, confess that techniques such as that described above have
proved more effective in the treatment of hysterical ailments, and
may even have some value with schizophrenia.

The layman's view is, as might be expected, a little different. An
Ibibio woman gave me the following account:

Though Christianity has come to us and driven some of these
evil practices away, but this particular one is still carried on by
wicked men and women of my countryside. Meetings are always
held in the midnight under a big cotton tree or in the market
when everyone is asleep. And there they discuss those whom
they will kill for the year. If you ask me, their main reason for
going on with this practice is so that they might be feared as
strong men and women, and to have a fat sum of money from
those who are worried by witchcraft before they are cured.

Anybody who starts to be suffering from the action of witches
is always very fat and nice to look at. Nobody when seeing them
can believe that the person is sick except people who are members of the witchcraft society. When it comes to the allotted
time to kill the person, that is, at the end of the year, the person

will have a fever or headache. People who do not know will think it to be malaria or a common fever, not knowing that the person is already dead. All medical aid will be given but in vain except the person is rushed to a native doctor who will reveal the whole secret and know whether the person will live or not. A native doctor who is a non-member of a witchcraft society cannot cure this sickness.

The native doctor will ask the parents of the sick person to buy the following things: a white cock that crows, a big goat, one yard of red and white cloth, one cup of rice to be cooked, seven shillings, seven sixpences, seven threepences, seven pennies and seven ha'pennies, one new spoon, one new plate and one bamboo table to be made for holding the food when going to the forest. When these things are brought, the native doctor will pack them all in to one big basin. When it comes to twelve o'clock midnight, the basin will be carried to the patient for sacrifice in the big forest and the patient must move with only a piece of cloth on the waist to cover his or her privates. The law to the patient is that nothing should make him or her turn back when they return from doing the sacrifice. (This is where the tricks always come from the native doctor who has made the sacrifice. The rule is that the patient after sacrifice must go in the front, followed by a relative and the native doctor to be the last, so that he might know the best part to play with that money without the knowing of the others.) When the forest is reached, the doctor will pass those things on the table as is the custom. My greatest surprise is that if witchcraft will no longer be worrying the person, both the goat and the fowl will die there without being killed by anybody, and all of them will return home in orderly fashion, and there will be no more sickness after three days.

There is a charming combination of trust (with regard to the therapy), and scepticism (with regard to motivation) in this story. Readers, however, may be left with some confusion as to who were the witches and who the doctors.

A woman may inherit a practice from her father if there are no sons, or sometimes if he thinks she is specially suitable, as in the delightful story of the reluctant sorceress.

It is also only too easy to become the wife of a doctor, whether one wishes to or not. Doctors willingly accept children as payment for services. Patients unable to pay immediately will temporarily pawn one of their offspring and quite often lack the means to redeem the child.

The following story was given me by a woman who had afterwards taken to the 'free life' rather than re-marry:

> I was seriously sick when I was in Standard Four. So my parents had to hand me over to a native doctor for treatment. The doctor looked after me till I recovered from sickness. The arrangement was that if I became well, my parents will pay him the sum of seven pounds, ten shillings and one goat. Failing to pay the agreed amount, the native doctor should claim me as a wife, provided my life was saved. When I recovered, my parents had not got the money to pay, so the man claimed me in return for his money. I did not enjoy the marriage because the man was old and dirty and all my school mates were laughing at me but I had to endure it because of my parents. In two years I became a 'very old woman'. I was even 'older' in appearance than my husband, because of heavy thoughts and much work. I worked for my mistress, who was his senior wife, and remained there till he died in 1959.

A patient may pawn himself or his wife if forced by poverty or childlessness. Traditionally, this was part of the slave economy, but now that the institution has in most senses been abolished, the pawn is usually a girl-child who, when of age, becomes a wife. The status of such a wife is to some degree ambiguous; she may be treated as a senior wife's servant or have less privileges than a woman for whom dowry has been paid. One is led to perceive some continuum between marriage and slavery—the nature of the relationship being without doubt dependent upon the power of the bride's father.

A grave hazard of marrying into a medical family is mentioned in one wife's story, in which the husband a kind of Ibibio Bluebeard, achieves his cures by means of the human sacrifice of his little pawn-wives. But whether this was traditional practice or a unique case of villainy, or the slander of a bitter woman, I leave to the reader's discernment.

A woman may, if she has the vocation, become a 'full diviner', combining all the occult and medical functions. Or she may be a priestess either of a specifically feminine cult, or as the custodian of her family's gods, if there is an absolute shortage of suitable men in her family. (Incidentally, a woman's family is that of her father. She never speaks of her husband and children as her family, as would an Englishwoman. Also, if we are to believe the emphasis of these stories, a girl's best friend is her uncle.)

Twenty per cent of the native doctors we interviewed were women, and it is interesting that in contrast to the men, none of them made grandiose claims, but confined themselves on the whole to headaches, diarrhoea and mild fevers. The men claimed cures for most disabilities, including bad luck, a tendency to steal, an unretentive memory for exams and the usual problems surrounding sterility. Leprosy and tuberculosis were treated until their cure was 'prohibited by the government'.

Reasons for entering the profession were given as:

(a) inheritance from parent   40%
(b) desire to revenge death of parent   10%
(c) acceptance of vocation after vision, visitation or seizure   20%
(d) apprenticeship from choice   12%
(e) apprenticeship following cure   18%
(f) apprenticeship after failure in other trades   15%

It may be seen that several have given more than one of these reasons.

The women spoke highly of 'western' medicine, and hospitals. Most men claim equal powers with European-trained doctors except with regard to surgery for which they professed admiration.

The only other profession open to the Ibibio peasant woman of this particular generation would appear to be that of midwife, which is of so little importance that it sometimes goes unmentioned, except by the interviewer.

In early anthropological works, and mission histories, there seems to be a tradition of Ibibio women warriors, but the period of this book is that of the *pax Britannica*, when such opportunities were temporarily closed.

I myself believe that this legend was based on a misinterpretation of one of the activities of the members of the women's society, Iban Isong, who, while their husbands were engaged in battle, used to perform a ritual war dance in male attire, either intended as sympathetic magic to aid the men, or to give an impression to other enemies that the warriors had not left the village.

I think the unique quality of the comparatively brief colonial period of peace and its effect on women's lives in particular, should not be forgotten. Not many of my old wives' tales are of the kind to stir one to feeling of feministic rage such as undoubtedly do the anecdotes of cruelty and exploitation found in Mrs Amaury Talbot's *Woman's Mysteries of a Primitive People*, which deals with the same tribe barely one generation earlier. The Ibibio women of Mrs Talbot's period were already approaching the colonial administrators to seek redress for the injustices forced upon them by their menfolk. By the time the next generation of girls became wives, many of the atrocities had been purged from customary marriage, and the remaining system is not without value and dignity.

The British administration not only safeguarded women from the worst tyrannies of their masters, it also enabled them to make their long journeys to farm or market without armed guard, secure from the menace of hostile neighbours. Thus by sheer hard work, the women of this generation have amassed a certain economic power, to some extent resented by their menfolk, who have by the same rule been deprived of a source of wealth in the spoils of war. Nevertheless, the good Ibibio wife was like the good Hebrew wife of the Old Testament, and her labours provided the prosperity of her husband and children. The Nigerian novelists who have written the charming and bucolic accounts of domestic harmony in African rural communities, are the sons whom the labours of these women educated; the peaceful village of their childhood to which they nostalgically look back was one which had been purged of bloodshed and alcoholism by an ague-ridden district officer and a Scottish mission lassie whose years were cut short by every kind of intestinal parasite.

It is even true to say that one of the most nostalgically convincing of the rural African novelists used as his source-book not the memories of his grandfathers but the records of the despised British anthropologists. A creative artist has the right to choose his Holinshead, but in this case, the anthropologist who was thought trustworthy as a source was also a District Officer such as this young writer invariably depicted as a buffoon incapable even of learning the vernacular. The result is that the modern African mythmaker hands down a vision of colonial rule in which the native powers are chivalrously viewed through the eyes of the hard-won liberal tradition of the late Victorian scholar, while the expatriates are shown as schoolboys' black-board caricatures.

26

The young African intellectuals choose to ridicule these people rather than the gun-boat and the factory in the creek which backed the pioneers from their position of comparative security; but one hears little ridicule or criticism from their mothers.

The one major criticism of colonial rule in this collection comes from a woman who complains bitterly of the leniency of British law, which allows a criminal to pass his days in the comfort and security of prison while his capital accumulates at home.

Mrs Talbot found a similarly appreciative reaction from the women of her day, as she writes in this heartfelt passage:

> That something of the beauty of the nature symbols which they worship enters into the character of the race however dimly felt or understood, is shown, I venture to think, by many an unexpected trait, and more especially by the touching gratitude evinced by some of the women, as well as by the humbler members of the community generally, at my husband's efforts to soften, as far as may be, the hardness of their lot. Time after time, attempts made upon his life in revenge for the punishment of evil practices were frustrated by warnings given, at the peril of their own lives, by such humble members of the race.

Even if we regard those 'evil practices' which Mrs Talbot condemns as inevitable consequences of overpopulation, it is impossible to deny that they were a cause of excruciating human suffering, and that women and children, being of lowest rank, were the greatest sufferers.

A marked feature of these women is their obvious gratitude for the opportunity to work; I have never heard it described as a hardship; rather is the lack of lands to farm bewailed, or the exacting culinary demands of their husbands which were eagerly passed on to a junior wife. Surplus farm-land meant not only a well-fed family but also crops to market. Market profits meant the purchase of additional lands (despite all customary laws forbidding such purchase), or the labour of young men. Eventually, it meant school fees, a festive 'coming-out' for her daughter, and the buying of traditional titles for husband, son or brother. A woman who could do all this within her lifetime was well contented with her lot.

But such fulfilment was only possible if she meanwhile overcame all the natural and man-made hazards with which her life was fraught from birth to death. Let us now enumerate some of these.

The Ibibio child enters this world by a gateway already distorted by the practice of female circumcision; once arrived, its chances of survival are again reduced (if the child of traditional parents) by rigid standards of conformity in infant acceptance.

I do not wish to appear over-critical of infanticide, which may in many cases be viewed as an heroic correction of biologic accidents, and might well be emulated by those who prefer the perpetuation of human misery to the soiling of their own hands by adult decision-making. The ethics of infanticide are relative to ecological and social conditions; some nations abandoning children they cannot support, and others children unlikely to be able to support them. The agricultural warrior-tribes of the Niger Delta were in the second category, ruthlessly weeding out abnormalities which they considered would prevent the development of a healthy adult soldier, hunter or farmer, though simultaneously discarding deviants whom we should regard as normal.

Survival of the average must long have supplanted survival of the fittest among most African peoples of the West Coast, who have practised the discarding of infants with even minor physical deviations since time immemorial. One is tempted to speculate to what extent human evolution has been moulded by such a practice which, for all we know, may have been prehistorically universal. In parts of West Africa, infanticide affects not only the newborn, for children late in walking, or cutting their top teeth before their lower ones, also risk exposure. The most conspicuous instance, and the one most publicized by outraged missionaries, was that of twin-birth. The custom of exposing twin-babes in clay pots in unhallowed portions of the forest, sometimes accompanied by their disgraced mother, is a well-known feature of pre-Christian Africa, although certain minority groups received them with especial welcome.

It would seem probable that twin-exposure belongs to the most markedly patriarchal and patrilineal clans and is not found in the matrilineal groups; I do not think the principle behind this is an especial aversion for multiple births among fathers, but rather that both infanticide and extreme patriarchy stem from the same cause: the social stress of famine.

To this day, in many areas, twin births terrify the uneducated, and are often considered sufficient cause for divorce. It is less well known that a surviving or rescued twin, if a girl, bears a life-long stigma. It is considered a serious insult to say of a man that he is capable of

marrying a twin-girl, and no woman will accept her as a co-wife.
There are various explanations given for this tabu, one that the
mother has had dealings with an evil spirit, who is father to one of
the children; another is the simpler criticism that it reduces a human
to the level of a dog or goat. It is rightly believed that twin-daughters
inherit a tendency to bear twins, but this stigma, like that of childlessness, is considered to have no bearing on fathers.

I feel that I must include at this point a moving biography given
me by an Ibibio woman of one of the twins rescued by the unfor-
gettable Mary Slessor, who is here remembered as an actual native
of Okoyong, and is naïvely pictured as striding through the bush
between Ibibioland and the Middle-Western region, followed by her
ambulance and men.

This man was born in the Mid-West Region in the year 1922.
His father was a native doctor with four wives. As a rule in those
days, any native doctor whose wife or wives deliver twin children,
such a wife or wives must not be allowed to enter the husband's
residence any longer as a wife. This law was kept for years by
our great fore-fathers in so much that nobody on earth can alter
it. Another law to this was that if such a wife is not allowed to
continue with the husband, the twins also must not be taken by
the father. In those days, they had one thick forest into which
such people were carried alive and also with the twins. As the
father to this man had four wives, his love with them was not
equally shared. To be very frank he had more love and liking
to the mother of this young man as she was the last wife to him.
So the other three women were then against the mother of this
young man. This woman also was not so fortunate to have
issues immediately she entered into the married home. But still
the husband was not interested. Fortunately for the mother of
this man, she was pregnanted at the seventh year of her stay with
the father of this man. The husband was very happy and he
showed his happiness to his well wishers both in manner and in
deeds. But to other co-wives of this lady, the happiness was
greatly spoiled within them. They all reasoned together of what
to do so that the pregnanted woman might no longer enjoy the
married home. Three of them arrived at the conclusion that they
should consult another native doctor who will make juju for the
woman to born twins so that the husband might no longer

continue with her as a husband. This was done and it really came
true. When the month was due for this lady to deliver, the
husband was very happy and prepared as he could for the new-
born baby. Very unlucky to him, his beloved wife delivered
twins. To obey the law, the woman had to be driven out from
the compound to the forest where people like that are being
killed. When the woman was taken to the forest, she was well
tied in one of the big trees there in the forest and the two children
were kept inside a big basin in front of the mother. As this
practice was very common in those days, there was a certain
woman who had been touring from place to place to save lives
of such mothers with their children who are being punished in
like manners because of delivering twins that God has given to
them. This famous Christian was born in Okoyong in the Old
Calabar Province. As this practice became too much, the woman
had to leave her home town to so many places that she heard that
the practice was still on. And the name of this woman as you
would like to know was called 'Mary Slessor'. So as Mary
Slessor was walking beside the forest where this woman was kept,
she heard the children crying. Slessor immediately entered the
forest without fear and saw this woman being tied in a tree with
the children in her front. One child had already died and the
other was still alive and that was the one we are now going to
hear of his life. Slessor quickly ordered her men to carry the
woman to the ambulance on the way with the child. Both the
mother and the remaining child were rushed to Okoyong where
the hospital was opened by Slessor for such people. In this
hospital, both the mother and her son were well cared for till the
mother became healthy and was able to give her own history to
the public. Slessor cared for the child till he reached a boy of
six years. He was made to start his class one infant in the Mission
School there at Okoyong where he passed his first school-leaving
certificate examination in the year 1935. He was given a scholarship for his six years' course in the Secondary School as it was
by then. Luckily when he passed his final examination; he was
employed at the Akpap Central school still within the area.
There in the teaching field, he got admission also. All tried that
they could to see that their son was to be one of the students
there as well. The Mission even were very happy in doing whatever is needed by the young man for him so that people when

seeing these types of children, they might not continue again with their evil belief, because the real parents of this man believed that if twins are allowed to be carried into the family, all members of the family will die. In 1945, he got into the University for his course. He was there for five years and had his M.A. degree. He returned back to Okoyong and he was later employed as a Principal in the Hope Waddell Institute Calabar. He remained there for years till the year his adopted mother died and that was Slessor. When Slessor died this man decided to leave his job to go and find job just in the very district that Slessor was buried. With this idea so many people were against it but he himself did not like to change his mind. And Slessor also was buried two hundred miles from her home town Okoyong. In short, she died in another province altogether and there she was buried.

So when this man remembered how he came to become a native in Okoyong instead of Burutu in the Mid-West, he really decided to leave his job and go and stay where Slessor was buried at Itu in Annang Province. All the efforts to change the man's mind was in vain. So in 1955, he resigned from the Hope Waddell to go and stay at Itu the place Slessor was buried by Christians when she was dead. When he reached there he gave his own story to people of that place. He asked the natives to sell a piece of land to him where he can set up his own building. The natives gave him a free land to set up his building. When he completed the building in 1957, he was appointed the Minister of the Methodist Church which Slessor opened at Itu. He set up a tomb of Slessor's image at where she was buried. He has a wife with three children now. He is now one of the Ministers spreading the word of God in the old Calabar and Annang Provinces as a whole.

That discarded infants, and sometimes their mothers, should be exposed in a part of the forest used for no other purpose, instead of being swiftly despatched and buried, is not wilful cruelty but the method usually believed to prevent either reincarnation or haunting And fortunately, as in classical times, childless parents still exist willing to ignore prejudice and regard a babe found by the wayside as a gift from God. Such a one became the beloved foster mother of one twin-woman who tells her story in these pages.

Before leaving the often distressful subject of infanticide, a little might be added from an ethological angle to justify the practice among primitive human groups. I do not believe any of the African peoples can be described as primitive, but the extreme hardship under which they have continued the complex life-styles of their ancestors has reduced them in many cases to the observance of basic and elementary laws of survival which may well parallel those of earlier antiquity. The custom of destroying one twin, which is usually the case even when two are exposed, and the custom of despatching infants born before the weaning of an elder sibling, may be viewed as remnants of primitive habits of sound biological basis in small, nomadic herds where infants must be carried, and freedom from predators must be bought by eternal vigilance.

Centuries of increasing safety and sophistication will cover such behaviour-patterns with mythologizing and highly imaginative rationalizing until the original purpose was forgotten while a continuity of emotional pressure to conform persists. For example, a forest dweller found to be sensibly rubbing his body with an insect-repellant balm made from specially gathered herbs, will explain that it brings 'good luck'. The necessity for the action has been passed on from generation to generation, while at some stage the explanation has been lost.

There still remain, under the harsh conditions of subsistence farming, excellent reasons for spacing of births and for considering twin-birth a disaster. The better organized ethnic groups traditionally solved the first problem by segregating the parents during the period of lactation—a situation not unduly disruptive in a polygynous household. Twin-birth remains—under a certain economic level—an almost insoluble dilemma. Missionaries who succeeded in saving the lives of twin children were formerly left without any alternative to bringing them up in their own households. Prosperity rather than moral change now safeguards the lives of twins.

The little Ibibio girl, after having passed the age threatened by infanticide, will for the next few years face only natural perils while she lives in her mother's cottage. However, if malaria or one of the seasonal epidemics takes her, it may well be suspected that she has been bewitched or poisoned by a childless wife of her father, though the suspicion would have been greater had she been that more envied possession—a son. The household skills she will be taught during these mainly carefree years are well within her power, if we exclude some overburdening with head-loads.

Until her period of seclusion when sexual education will traditionally be imparted, the only teaching unconcerned with household duties received by the child will be in the form of fairy-tales, cautionary tales, and historical legend, and above all a perpetual bombardment with proverbial wisdom. An attentive child need not lack culture. Even with regard to the household tasks, a fairly elaborate ritual of hygiene and courtesy must be learned and good mannerliness is highly prized in the young.

The little girl will early learn to cook, and will carry her father's meals to him where he eats alone or with a favoured son in his own house; but she will return to eat with her mother in her apartment.

Not merely the segregation of feeding but also the manner in which food is shared out, are significant aspects of the life-style of any people.

If we are to take seriously the findings of modern ethology in its application to the basic behaviour-patterns of human populations, the civilized ritual of the Efik-Ibibio peoples, in its present fragmented state, interspersed with brutal hierarchical conduct, is indicative of the collapse of a higher unrecorded culture undermined by the traumatic shocks of warfare and famine. Typical of these degenerate interspersions is the system of food-sharing according to domestic rank, i.e. brute strength, rather than need. This pattern, by which the male head takes the lion's share of any protein-containing food and children are fortunate to receive a bone as a reward, is common to most of tropical West Africa. This is so fully established in custom as to be totally ritualized with agreed punishments for the concealment by the wife of any portion of the food. That there has been in recent times some slight improvement is indicated by the assumption by the men that the women may with impunity and often do give their allotted share to the children. However, food-stealing (from one's own family) is still considered one of the worst juvenile crimes. An Ibibio proverb is still in use: 'To the beloved, the father giveth meat with the bone.'

This conduct pattern has no relation to racial character, or even innate human greed, but has been observed to be one of the inevitable results among mammalian populations, who normally cherish their young, of severe stress from hunger and/or overcrowding. That hunger was most certainly the case is shown almost heart-rendingly by the commonest form of ritualized Ibo greeting, which is roughly translated thus:

'How is it with you and your family?'
'Fine thanks. No worries except hunger.'
'Good. Hunger is better than sickness.'

It is unlikely that the Ibibios, living under almost identical circumstances, fared differently.

The chances are, unfortunately, that the child will not mature by her mother's side, but will be sent, as a little apprentice wife, into the home of her mother-in-law, who, in her son's interest, will train her more rigorously than did her mother. The years a girl spends as a little cinderella figure in the household of her future husband are seldom her happiest, but she is at least well protected and her patience is sometimes rewarded when her husband notices that she has become a beautiful young woman. Then she may return any slights and injustices she has suffered when serving her senior co-wives. This of course is hardly conducive to domestic harmony.

A husband who has been unable to refrain from making a woman of the child-wife beneath his roof may wish, nevertheless, to spare her the danger of too early childbirth. A strange story is told in the following collection by a wife who remained childless forever because her husband laid a spell on her to prevent pregnancy, then died before removing it.

Polygyny is another traditional African institution considered worthy of criticism by the Missions, though by no means to the same degree as infanticide. Moreover two generations of peace and increasing prosperity during British rule served to undermine the two pillars of demographic imbalance and privation which gave the custom its security. Critics therefore felt justified by the disharmony which was becoming more obvious in such families to label polygamy as unnatural in comparison with the 'nuclear' family of Britain and America.

However, it would seem clear from these old wives' tales that those women least touched by western civilization were willing to accept the inner logic of a system where perennial tribal skirmishing by creaming off the young warriors made nonsense of a rule of 'one man, one wife'; and where heavy labour in farm and market could make a welcome helpmeet of the person who would be a sexual rival in more clement circumstances.

The educated and progressive wives in this series, and many of the daughters of the traditional women, are already taking advantage of the increasing number of marriageable youths to endorse the Mission view of Christian marriage as a monogamic companionship of equals; but the older women who consider themselves to have been happily married, seem satisfied with their share in a patriarch whom they have been able to respect, and his virtues as a father and wise counsellor are praised rather than his companionship and love.

Among the grand-daughters of these old wives, we find a class of moderns who are bitterly antagonistic to the patriarchal attitude of their rural ancestors: young professionals to whom the idea of supporting a husband from their income as did their mothers is so repugnant that they prefer to remain unwed while nevertheless bearing children whom they place with their relatives for upbringing. (But that was in pre-war Nigeria; and now, presumably, the wheel has gone full circle.)

Sometime between babyhood and maturity most African women experience an acute source of suffering, which may also be dangerous, namely female circumcision. Among the Efik people, who are closely related to the Ibibio, this operation may be carried out as early as at one year old, but not later than fifteen, but it is never omitted. Among the Ibibio themselves, who are less conservative, the wearing of clothes has made the omission of this custom less conspicuous and it is said to be dying out. However, I think we may safely assume that the generation of women who contributed to this book all endured this painful ceremony and, in their tradition, it would take place at maturity, before a woman was officially released to her husband. There is little actual mention of the operation in these stories. Converted women soon learned from the Missions that certain subjects were not spoken about by ladies and they restrict themselves to telling of the fattening ceremony which was the usual form of convalescence after surgery.

Modern Ibibio ladies whom I have questioned describe their form of circumcision as clitoridectomy, but some European doctors have queried this on the grounds that the actual excision of the clitoris would result in the prevention of several natural functions. Nevertheless, we have the following account from one Ibibio woman:

The traditional purpose of circumcising girls was to prevent
the clitoris from standing out, and to have been circumcised

meant that a girl was a completely beautiful or full woman. She was, in addition to that, fit for the woman's society known as Iban Isong, organized in the village. There was also a rude gesture which could be understood as meaning that one at whom it was made was uncircumcised; and if by mistake this gesture was made to a woman who, according to this tradition, was completely beautiful, she had the right to sue the offender in the court of the woman's society. The offender, if proved guilty, was punished beyond imagination.

Since the rite was a public matter, the woman whose outgrowing clitoris was never cut off became an object of ridicule before her contemporaries. She would make the greatest mistake to provoke a quarrel, for she would have the worst part of her opponent's tongue.

This informant tells us that in Oron-Calabar areas,

circumcision was usually a ceremonious affair. The girl's mother must publish this matter. This practice usually follows a little peace offering, asking for the protection of any deity from dangerous bleeding. There are usually some drinks, and this is wholly and solely a women's matter. After the circumcision and the drinks, the girl stays in her own private apartment for treatment and she eats much more than usual. In a month's time, she is healthy and fatter than usual. Her outing is then ceremonious; the parents buy clothes, shoes and ornaments, and she goes out to the church if of Christian parents, or otherwise she goes round the market where she collects presents.

A less impersonal account was given by a charming and sophisticated Ibo air hostess, incidentally a devout and practising Roman Catholic, who when at boarding school had wished for what she regarded as a 'coming-out' ceremony in order to be like other girls. So she wrote home to her village and asked her parents to arrange this, which they did with considerable expense and publicity. Much to her chagrin, she found that the celebration was one at which she did not attend, being at this time laid out on a banana-leaf behind the house in considerable agony, her wounds having been cauterized in the traditional manner, with pepper. This lady commented that the pains of childbirth such as she experienced in later years were mild in comparison with the pain of that day.

The aesthetic explanation of female circumcision given by the Ibibios seems to me a somewhat tautological rationalization. Other peoples give other reasons for this ritual. One traditional excuse is that it assists childbirth. This is demonstrably false, as far as literal interpretations go, since the scar-tissue left by the operation cannot stretch and must make tearing inevitable. However, if the statement is taken as a reference to ritual significance, it may be the truest explanation of why the operation is performed.

A well-known theory is that circumcised women are protected from temptation to infidelity by the discomfort of intercourse. A modern Nigerian mother of three small daughters gave as a reason for subjecting them to this torture that it would spare them the sin of sexual pleasure. She also was a devout Christian and felt that the practice harmonized with her religious beliefs. To this explanation I can only say that it does not seem to have worked that way: native history and legend are crowded with unfaithful wives.

In Nigeria, female circumcision is in fact illegal, and also forbidden by the Church. Nevertheless, girls continue to be brought into hospital, ill and sometimes dying from badly performed operations.

Although this festival is one that can only be enjoyed by the older female relatives of the central character involved, and then only if they are hard-hearted enough to turn a deaf ear to her screams, 'fattening', on the other hand, is regarded as a happy and proud occasion for mother and daughter alike.

Accorded to the tradition recounted by Mrs Amaury Talbot, a girl whose parents could afford the expense was secluded in the 'fattening house' on three occasions, but I believe that the early ceremony—like the circumcision of female infants—was mainly confined to the Efiks. The women I have interviewed have experienced only one fattening, or else their memory has run together all the occasions, which seems unlikely, as the event is usually recalled as one of the few interesting things that have happened to them.

The experience of solitary confinement, with no more activity than the intensive consumption of carbohydrates, together with a little massage and the application to the body of oil and clay—and this lasting for at least three months, but occasionally for as much as three years (and in this case considered a great privilege)—would not be judged by most European women as the ideal way to spend one's teen-age. But, presumably, if one thought that no other way existed of acquiring the qualities necessary to be sought after in marriage and admired and accepted by one's society, one would enter the fattening house as gladly as 'civilized' women endure the discomfort and boredom of the beauty salon. Early women travellers have deplored the expression of self-satisfaction and vanity with which the fattening-house girls emerge from seclusion to face the admiration of the assembled villagers, but how can one condemn this short hour of innocent glory in a life of almost total dedication to the service of the family?

The displeasing facial expression of the fattened girls may also reflect the illusion of power which may come to them as a result of the temporary cessation of their usual state of subservience. For this short period a girl may ask for anything; she may be carried, like a chief; all people must make her offerings as if she were a chief; so she may wear the arrogant air of a chief, which does not blend well with youthful ignorance.

There is in fact a curious parallel between the Eastern Nigerian's fattening of maidens and the coronation of tribal kings in other parts of West Africa, for which those who engage in such rituals can give no explanation.

How it feels to be fattened and fêted is sufficiently described in the old wives' tales in this book, so I shall restrict myself to some interpretations of this interesting custom. I think we may dismiss the explanation which comes most readily to an expatriate on first encountering this system, namely that daughters are fattened for sale, like cattle for the market. Firstly, prospective husbands very often contribute to the cost of fattening their fiancées, having already accepted them in their natural state of thinness. Secondly, the fattening may be carried out in the husband's home if it has been omitted before marriage.

The connection between fatness and beauty is not as many expatriates believe, typically African. A survey of personal aesthetics among villagers showed that a woman buxom enough to denote health while slender enough to move gracefully was the ideal, as undoubtedly it has always been among peoples unburdened by excessive sartorial demands. The Ibibio priestess of these stories considered her pathological fatness to be disgraceful, and apparently it was horrifying to her family.

There is an undoubted connection between fattening and convalescence after circumcision. When they do not actually coincide, they are nevertheless identical in procedure. Another interesting phenomenon is that the girls exposed after fattening either are, or appear to be, in an advanced state of pregnancy.

There are some customs in Nigeria which are not mentioned directly but which often come up in legal disputes over divorce or breach of promise. One of these is that the fertility of a bride must be demonstrated before she is regarded as marriageable. A legal wrangle which occupied the Port Harcourt press for many months recently concerned a West Indian nurse who supported a young Nigerian during his studies in Britain on the understanding that he would marry her on return to his own country. This unfortunate lady discovered on arrival in Africa that she was not the only female guest in his house, and that no wedding was forthcoming. When she sued him not only for breach of promise but also for the monies she had spent on his education his reply was that she had shown no signs of pregnancy during all the time they were together. When she replied indignantly that of course she had taken natural precautions, it was generally agreed that this was not good behaviour on the part of a prospective bride and she lost her case.

In the light of such cases and the fact that among numerous African peoples, marriage is preceded by a visit to the prospective husband's compound, after which pregnancy must be demonstrated before the marriage can be finalized, I think we must seriously consider 'fattening' as either an actual or symbolic declaration of fertility. We must also remember that customary marriage has no wedding, but takes place in various stages of instalments. (The first stage or betrothal may take place before the birth of the bride, the 'engagement ring' being inscribed upon the mother's tummy.)

Mrs Talbot, in describing the three Efik fattenings, explains that the last two are separated by a visit to the husband's house, after which the bride returns, to seclusion in her parents' compound, possibly for three years. Now it is common all over West Africa for husbands to send wives back to their mothers for childbirth and the period of lactation—roughly three years if we include pregnancy—so it seems to me that Mrs Talbot has not been given the whole story, or that a lady of her delicacy, who invariably described puberty simply as the place where brook and river meet, could not bring herself to interrogate her informants concerning the physiological basis of this segregation.

One clue to the significance of the clitoridectomy-fattening complex is the fact that if these ceremonies have not already taken place by the time an engaged girl becomes pregnant—whether in her parents' or in her husband's home—they are often rushed, so that they can be completed before the birth, even though this is known to be a risky procedure. The whole syndrome is in fact relevant to childbirth, although it is normally arranged to coincide with the agricultural ceremonies.

There is one aspect of the fattening ceremony which understandably has not been openly discussed with missionaries or ethnographers, and that is its part in the wider group activity of sacrifice to the goddess of fertility. This may largely be a forgotten connection; but it is noticeable that the maidens are traditionally fattened in groups and at a particular season and that the spilling of blood from the sexual parts upon the newly tilled soil is a commonplace of fertility ritual in all parts of the world where such rites have been recorded. That the part should eventually come to be substituted for the whole person as a sacrifice to demanding but easily duped deities is a frequent event in the early history of many cultures.

I have included fattening among the hazards which face Ibibio girls because, although apparently enjoyable, it is dietetically unhealthy. Applications to the skin intended to prevent loss of weight through sweating are also ill-advised in such a climate. We hear in this book of girls dying in the fattening-house during epidemics, and it is quite likely that this way of life increased their vulnerability.

Fattening is followed, if not preceded, by marriage, which has its own hazards.

In pre-Christian times, probably the most severe risk for the woman in the married state was the suspicion of witchcraft. The orthodox African, though surrounded by nature spirits, was no believer in natural causes. Unwished-for happenings were invariably attributed to human agency, and the person chosen for suspicion was usually the one least able to retaliate when taken to trial. This does not reflect on the evil character of the pre-literate native, but rather on general human gullibility, as the strategy of the witch-hunt in Africa varied only in detail from that which has been the shame of most civilized peoples at some period of their history. Nor, I hasten to add, does this practice prove anything about the 'stupidity' of the black man—rather the reverse—for those diviners who conducted the African witch trials were as unscrupulously brilliant as any white inquisitor directing an *auto-da-fé*.

In pre-Mission days, and in rural areas until much later, the death of a Nigerian chief was sufficient to send every mobile local person below a certain social status into hiding, since he would be in peril either as a suspected regicide or even if innocent, he might by tradition be expected to accompany his lord to the nether regions. But suspected, and usually innocent, assassins were invariably found and brought to trial, and the bereaved family of the chief had to pay the diviner heavily for these scapegoats, otherwise they themselves would stand in grave danger of accusation.

With regard to causes of witch trials, a continuum existed in importance from the death of a chief, down to the febrile convulsion of the youngest daughter of the next to the poorest man in the land. (The poorest man, naturally, could not afford the costs of the procedure.) A parallel continuum of suitable suspects obtained, and way down at the bottom of the pecking order of scapegoats would be presumably the youngest daughter of the sickliest slave of the ugliest wife of the poorest man in the land, but such a person would be out of the running since she would be unable to pay the diviner who not invariably incremented his fees by doubling as counsel for the defence. Also, certain classes of slaves were outside prosecution, as belonging to a deity and therefore officially 'dead'. So the best choice of suspect for the least important case would most likely be the envied childless favourite wife of the father of the sick child. A woman of this category may walk in fear and dread until the birth of a son puts an end to her insecurity. Such a wife tells her own story in the following pages.

As in the civilized world until deplorably recent times, the suspected witch in pre-Christian Ibibioland was not usually suffered to live; and though in the commonest form of trial—namely ordeal by poison— the accused could pay the diviner to serve up the ingredients in a digestible and non-lethal form, it was in the latter's interest to prove guilt by killing the 'witch'.

It is perhaps fortunate that the colonial occupation of Nigeria took place at the height of the feminist movement in Britain, when the thoughts of consuls and missionaries were centred on situations of sexual injustice. Present-day Africans fulminate in their newspapers on the sins of the Imperialists, one of the worst of which was the emancipation of African women. The full effect of this is of course limited to the educated and city dwellers. Implicit obedience can still be demanded of the country wife, but is less likely to be enforced by such dire threats as previously. Similarly, the witch-hunt, though still common, may nowadays end in the disgrace or divorce of an innocent person, but not usually her execution. Most of the serious dangers inherent in the system of customary marriage, whether from parent, husband, or jealous co-wife, had already been eliminated by the time about which the old ladies in this book are writing. The *justice* of the system belongs to a different argument and a different book. Suffice it to say that most traditionally married women did not themselves condemn the system, though the few who adopted new habits criticize the conservatism of their sisters.

The ritual of the Ibibio marriage requires some description and explanation.

As in the case of most of the coastal or Rivers peoples, the expenses of Ibibio marriage are not inflated or exorbitant. It is roughly estimated that in pre-military independent Eastern Nigeria, the costs to the bridegroom's family of Ibibio-Efik ceremonies amounted to twenty-eight pounds, compared with twenty-six pounds among the Kalabari-Ijaw, and two-hundred and twenty-four pounds among the Ibos.

I think this may be taken to indicate a closer affinity to matrilinity (i.e. a tendency for wives to belong to their parents' family and be less permanently aligned to their husbands') among the coastal tribes, one reason for which could be the greater mobility of these people where the husband could travel by canoe throughout the massive network of inland waterways to trade or fish or set up a separate establishment; and the wife likewise could easily return to mother on any pretext. Actually a gradation of marriage exists among the Kalabari, by which a man can pay a higher dowry to the parents of a permanent wife and a lower one for a lady who may leave him after giving him a son.

The more land-bound Ibos of the interior, whether inclined to take a wife for better or for worse, must demonstrate their respect for a permanent alliance with the bride's family by payment of a mighty sum.

Tradition has it that in earlier days no bride-price was paid, and suitors did not need to identify themselves or their families, but that the custom arose because of incidents like the following:

Once upon a time, there was a beautiful girl named Mayen
who was so proud that she refused to marry any of the local boys
who asked for her hand.

However one day, a gorgeously dressed stranger took her fancy and her parents were so relieved that they allowed her to depart with him.

When they had gone a few miles, the stranger called at a house and returned the fine garments, which he had borrowed for the occasion. Although disturbed by this, Mayen followed him for many more miles until they came to his isolated and fortified compound.

When they entered into his house, the stranger told Mayen that she should have nothing to eat until she guessed his name. The next day he left to go hunting, after repeating his threat, and she spent the day walking around the compound and weeping.

The following day the same thing happened, and it was then that the skulls which littered the courtyard began to speak to her. They told her they had been his former wives, and at this Mayen began to weep bitterly, but could find no way to escape.

However, the skulls comforted her, advising her to assuage her hunger by eating some chalk which was in the house. After this, she took council with the former wives, and they told her that her wicked husband's name was Ntanti, the two-skinned man.

That evening when her husband returned, Mayen told him that she knew his name. But since his day's hunting had been unsuccessful, Ntanti could give her no food. On the contrary, he decided that on that day he would dine on poor Mayen.

Now Ntanti had a special place where he used to slaughter his wives, in a creek about five miles away, so he began to drag the unfortunate Mayen in that direction. However, she was a strong girl, and in her struggles caused him to lose his knife. Cursing, he tied her to a tree by the creek, and returned to fetch another knife.

It so happened that it was market day, and Mayen's three brothers were rowing their canoe along the creek from the market place when they heard her bewailing her fate. The elder brothers were for hastening home, fearing it was a ghost, but the younger brother swore it was the voice of his beloved sister. Nonsense, said the others, she is at present enjoying her husband. At last they decided to explore and taking their paddles for weapons, waded into the creek. They had no sooner found their sister than Ntanti's footsteps were heard returning. Quickly they hid in the bush, and as the villain raised his knife they leaped upon him, forced him to confess and then killed him.

Rejoicing, the boys carried home their rescued sister. And from that day her parents and their neighbours declared that no girl should leave home unless her suitor could demonstrate his respectability by proving his origins and depositing a substantial dowry.

Such marriages are conducted much as those of royal personages in Europe, and if custom is rigidly observed have no resemblance to the sale or purchase of slaves. Of course, insensitive parents exist in Nigeria as elsewhere, prepared to view the matter in a purely commercial light; they are not respected but neither are they punished, which is one of the faults of the system. Similarly, unscrupulous husbands marry the daughters of uninfluential men, knowing that no law exists to enforce respect of such wives, who can be slighted and overworked.

'Slave-wives' have existed in the recent past, as a separate category doubtless connected with a war economy. Certainly an important factor in the status of women has always been the status and proximity of their fathers. Also apparent from these stories is another sign of a matrilineal past: the care bestowed on a girl by her brother or her mother's brother. An Ibibio father can say to his daughter what seems to us a particularly heartless and hurtful thing. 'Why should I care for you as I do for my sons? A girl is like the seed of the oil-bean: when ripe she must be shot in the air and bear fruit where she lands.' This may well be because he does not feel absolute bonds of kinship with the females of his wife's line, whereas, on the other hand, a girl's brother or maternal uncle regards himself as her true relative.

Nevertheless, the Ibibios do not like their daughters to marry outside Ibibioland, which I think must be viewed as some concern for their welfare.

The fate of one Ibibio girl who strayed too far from her father's compound was described by her as follows:

The father of my child has no other wife but he is hoping to marry one girl from his town, because we are not from the same town. He is an Ibo man. He got me with child in 1961 while I was staying with my senior sister who is with her husband in this town. He came and gave my sister's husband who is my in-law some bottles of beer promising to go and see my parents after my delivery. Since then he has not made any idea of going to see my parents again. When I delivered the baby child to him, he had to go and register the child but still he made no idea of going to see my parents. When my sister went home during Christmas time she told him that I should go with her and see my people but he refused. At present I don't know what to do. I only wait for the day to come when he will marry his towns-girl; there and then will I carry my child and go, and leave the house for him and his wife. I see no reason why I will leave my child for him, while he is feeling that he cannot go and pay dowry on my behalf being a girl of another town. Anyway, I always separate from him to my sister each time we fight, because I always feel that it is a cheat for me to continue cooking for him by that time while he is treating me as though I am not a human being as he is. His brother who is an applicant always accompanies him to fight with me without minding whether I am holding a child at hand or not.

In Ibibioland, as in most of West Africa, evidence of a recent matrilineal way of life is clearly seen in the retention of many customs. For example, one story in this book is by a woman whose father retained her as a 'home-daughter' to continue his line through offspring fathered by a series of strangers. To be faithful to the tradition, this father should have provided her with a share of the farmland, but he preferred to exploit her as a source of revenue. As she bitterly comments, fathers have discovered that if they give their daughters land, they prefer to farm for their living rather than depend on 'lovers'. Thus the home-daughter falls between two traditions, and finds herself dispossessed and homeless in her old age.

Another matrilineal remnant, of which, unfortunately, I have no example in this book, is that of the heiress who, finding herself in sole charge of her property, chooses to take a wife rather than a husband. This is not in the least indicative of homosexuality, but simply a rational procedure aimed at continuing the family while keeping hold of her birthright. Either or both women will have children at their own discretion, dividing the labour of agriculture and domesticity between themselves.

An Ibibio remnant of something more than matrilineal custom, and which could even have some bearing on matriarchy—rare though that mythical state seems to be—is the ritual war dance of Eka

Akpan, the mother of the war-god. By some strange coincidence, Eka Akpan is also Eka Ekkpo, the mother of spirits, the great earth-goddess herself. Apparently, not only in her agricultural form but also as a war leader, this goddess must have originated among the women, since her ritual has to be carried out in female dress. Even to this day, men plait their hair and disguise themselves as women to serve Eka Akpan.

The choice of the first bride for a young man is mainly the work of his mother, who through visits and general gossiping will investigate the reputation for industriousness of girl-children in her vicinity. The wishes of the prospective bridegroom may be considered, and argument ensue if a pretty but unindustrious maiden has taken his fancy. This strife is not as serious as it would be in a monogamous society since the homely hardworking bride may so improve the young man's wealth that he may soon come to afford the second prettier one. After informal discussion has taken place between the mothers-in-law, the decisive action is in the hands of the prospective fathers-in-law. The groom's father will visit, taking drinks and presents, and it is acknowledged that he is 'marrying a wife for his son'. You will notice this expression in many of the stories, and it is a fair description of what traditionally happens, since although the bride is exclusively her husband's for the begetting of children, she is otherwise married to all of his family. Any of them, including younger siblings of either sex, address her as 'my wife'. Certainly she will not be setting up house alone and isolated like an English or American bride, even if she is the first wife of her husband. The 'compound' which she enters will be a group of single-roomed cottages clustered round that of the family head, whose dwelling is specially appointed to receive social calls, and where he takes his meals alone unless accompanied by a favourite child. If her husband is head of the household she will have a separate cottage, and her children will sleep there with her. But whether she is the wife of a chief or a youngest son, she will marry into an 'extended family' group in which she will hold a junior position, but where she need fear neither loneliness nor the terrifying novel problems of solitary motherhood.

For an expatriate accustomed to the squalor of the poor quarters of African towns, the sight of the orderly Nigerian village is a pleasant surprise. It is difficult not to be charmed by the circle of decorated cottages surrounding a well-swept glade, within the shadow of the mighty forest trees. A scrupulous Ibibio housewife will keep the floor and walls of her house scrubbed and polished, so that although much of the furnishing is made of compressed earth, no one can soil his garments on them. Her kitchen must always be neat. Her water-pots must go up on the shelf above the fireplace, her mortars must be cleaned and turned upside-down on a stone or a piece of flat wood. Her pestles must be hung up on slings, her plates washed and stored in a big basket. The water-pot in use is safely stood on a ring at a corner of the pantry. The woman's soul is related to her water-pot, and it is a sad humiliation for her to find it placed outside the compound, as this indicates her dismissal by her husband.

The first consultation of the father will be followed by others where the son attends and contributions may be made at this stage towards the young lady's fattening. All her family will receive presents according to seniority.

The groom must make several visits with increasing gifts to his fiancée's home. On no account must the decision or contract be concluded on one occasion, lest it be mistaken for an act of purchase. Parents are reasonably touchy on this matter. After a few return visits, the bride eventually makes her final departure, and if she is young and being married for the first time, it is very unlikely that her wishes will have been consulted throughout. She will not even be a very important participant at the celebrations. Women who have been married by customary law will usually describe themselves as having had no 'wedding', regarding the latter as a purely Christian phenomenon. With all this coming and going, it is quite difficult to say at which stage a woman is regarded as well and truly married, and I am inclined to believe those Ibibio men who have told me that a marriage is not considered consummated until there is definite proof of pregnancy. Certainly the wives in these stories are continually telling us that there is no such thing as divorce and in the next breath saying that their first husband divorced them for barrenness.

One informant told me of a final 'handing-over' ceremony at which the bride was escorted to her husband's home together with as many of the following items as her parents could afford (see list on following page).

This is clearly a slightly more modern version of the trousseau provided by her mother for the girl newly come out of the fattening room, as described in these stories; and since my informant tells me also that while the 'handing-over' was going on the baby was being

Household equipment	Estimated cost		
	£	s	d
Wooden Spoon		1	0
Broom		1	0
Plates	2	0	0
Iron Pots	3	0	0
Earthen Pots		10	0
Baskets		2	0
Goats (male and female)	3	0	0
Sewing Machine	20	0	0
Tables, chairs and mirrors	4	0	0
Jugs, tumblers and spoons	1	10	0
Iron Box and Damasks	10	0	0
	£44	4	0

looked after by its grandparents, I can only assume that fattening, marriage and childbirth involved overlapping and sometimes interchangeable rituals.

It is still traditional among many Nigerian peoples to send wives to their mothers for childbirth and the whole period of lactation, and townswomen are of two minds about the value of this; some saying how refreshing it is to return to the village of their youth, even to lie on the cool, hard, earthenware bed and to laze about, basking in their mother's care. Others grumble, saying that their husbands revive the custom out of stinginess, refusing to maintain them during that period as they would have to do in the city, and expecting them to support themselves by farming to which they are already unaccustomed.

However, in the days when these stories were written, one great advantage of returning to mother for childbirth was that the extreme vulnerability of the woman in labour could not then be exploited as an interrogation situation by her in-laws. It was apparently customary among many of the Nigerian peoples for the mother-in-law and other relatives to use the ignorance and terror of a young wife who is giving birth for the first time to extract confessions of sorcery or infidelity, telling her that the child will not come forth till she admits to whatever crimes they choose to accuse her of. The unfortunate woman is told that the infant is punishing her in the name of his father.

Even without such heaven-sent opportunities for in-laws to inflict torture while preserving 'clean hands', the fate of the mother in the tender care of well-wishers may be hard enough. She finds herself once more in the backyard on the traditional banana-leaf, her labour assisted by ceremonial chanting and a rigid routine which makes no allowance for complications. A British-trained Nigerian nursing sister gave me the following account of village methods of midwifery:

> With over 400 expectant mothers a year depending on her care for their confinement, with no knowledge of midwifery except what is passed on to her by her grandmother and a few local herbs and roots to rely on, this handy midwife moves about with great confidence and respect amongst the local people in the village.
>
> I dare say, it is this confidence in herself which often is lacking in our midwives today that makes her successful in most of her attempts to practise midwifery.
>
> As with most things however, she has had her faults and in some cases this has meant the loss of lives, mother and baby, or baby alone, and a very high rate of maternal disability.
>
> This indeed reminds me of my awful experience when I visited my village in 1956. I arrived home at about 3 p.m. in the company of my mother and son; the news went round that I was in town and in thirty minutes of our arrival men and women of my compound and distant relatives were gathering to see me. They were coming with gifts of all kinds, i.e. pots of palm wine from the men folks, basins of coco yam, coconuts and what have you from the women. Amongst these people, I noticed that the wife of a relative of whom I was very fond was missing from the crowd. After several enquiries it was revealed that she could not be there because she had been under labour for the past couple of days.
>
> On receiving this information I could no longer contain myself and as soon as the crowd dispersed I made straight for the compound where she lived wondering within myself what could be the reason for such delayed labour for a multiparous woman.
>
> On arriving to the scene I made for the back of the house where I was told I would find her. There I saw a group of women chanting songs which they explained would hasten the delivering and at the same time giving her bowls of concocted medicine all to hasten delivery. All by my observation made her look the more weak and her tummy was greatly distended. She indeed looked terribly worn out.
>
> After further enquiries I discovered that she had been out in

that open place and on the bare ground with a plantain leaf as her bed for the last two days and juice squeezed out of local herbs as her only food, for according to custom she is not supposed to go into the house nor have any food to eat until the baby is born. The story almost paralysed me and in great anger I dispersed all the women and the native midwife who was supposed to be conducting the delivery and who by my observation had given up hope of anything good coming out of Israel.

This poor lady as I said was very tired and could hardly move her limbs. She could not refuse me. I felt her pulse and glad that it was fairly satisfactory only showing sign of shock. With the help of her husband we moved her into her apartment. I gave her a quick wash down for she was practically covered with dust and sweat and covered her up for warmth. I managed to do a quick abdominal palpation and found the head of the foetus was still high for a multipare labour. This finding further proved that she had been whipped off to the back of the house with a false labour and made to push until she became quite exhausted.

Before long, I noticed that she was fast asleep, so I left her alone to rest as I felt that was what she needed most, in any case it is unlikely that she will deliver for another six to eight hours. With this opportunity I got ready everything I needed for her delivery. Some of these I had with me and some I borrowed from the nearby dispensary. When I came back after a couple of hours or so she was still sleeping, but she woke up in about an hour after my arrival and asked for a hot drink and we offered a small plate of pepper soup made with few pieces of yam and this she ate up as fast as it came. Not quite an hour after she asked for more and this time I gave her a small bowl of pap with plenty of milk and sugar. It was after this that I will say she recognized me and sat up to talk with me and with her husband who was then my only assistant in the business. The next thing that this lady asked for was to go to the toilet and I must say that I was very happy about this and quickly offered her an old bucket that I reserved for my dirty water during delivery. At first she refused to use it and insisted on going to the pit latrine. After much persuasion she consented to use the bucket. Everything was quiet from then on and it was 9 p.m. when I settled her down again and made myself comfortable on the next wooden bed and asked the husband to go off to his apartment, for there was no need for anxiety. In the next few minutes we were both off to sleep.

When she called me again, it was 2.30 a.m. by my watch. This time she said that she felt like going to the toilet again and also complained of pain. I knew that this time, she was truly in labour so I rushed out for the old bucket and by the time I came back she was pushing. I got things ready as quickly as I possibly could, tidied her bed and then encouraged her to push having cleaned her up. Soon the head of the foetus was seen and in less than another ten minutes the baby was born. The baby and I shouted for joy. It was a girl. The cry of the baby was so strong that I suppose it woke her husband who came flying into the apartment where we were. Soon he was dancing and shouting for joy and both his shouts and the cry of the baby brought the nearest neighbours in including my mother. Every place was full of joy. I was full of joy and I dare say my mother was very proud of me and all the women who were with her and had almost given up hope were very surprised at my achievements and started to pour praises on me.

Soon the mother and baby were ready to be seen. People came in hoards to see the miracle mother and baby. I was surprised at the number of people that came; little did I know that news of what had happened had spread through the whole town and they were coming to see for themselves. They brought with them all kinds of presents for the baby and mother and among the people that came from far off was the old native midwife who when she came shook my hand and congratulated me for the excellent job done.

As for the mother herself not to mention her husband, from then on they did not cease to thank me and to pour God's blessings on me.

Personally I felt very happy not because of my achievement but because of the lives saved and the splendid lesson which my people learnt from the occurrence. I thus gave them more confidence in the superiority of modern midwifery practice over primitive midwifery.

The sister who told that story is a queenly beauty with considerable prestige as an educated woman and a 'been-to', that is one who has finished her schooling abroad; otherwise she could not have been permitted to return her patient to her bed indoors. It is traditionally an outrageous defiance of tabu to defile house and bed by the unclean act of birth. In cases of normal delivery for a woman used to a hard couch, the banana-leaf in the open air is undoubtedly preferable to a stuffy windowless cottage in the tropical climate. However, the continuation of the tradition by townspeople accustomed to bedding and privacy has caused a curious impasse. It is surprising to a foreigner to find in the poorer urban districts of Nigeria a maternity-home at almost every street corner, catering for those who are not permitted to defile the sacredness of the Vono mattress. The conditions in these 'maternity-homes', as described by this same nursing-sister, are by no means an improvement on village methods.

Childbirth is the most significant advance in the Ibibio woman's life, and if she is fortunate enough to bear the first son of her husband, she is from then on assured of a certain degree of respect. As senior wife a woman has some status in the man's world, though she may be displaced by a favourite. But her status is chiefly relevant to the women's world where she has her traditional organization and rituals.

The senior wife in an African household is often considered to be the only true wife, who may join her husband in certain official ceremonies. Traditionally, she should be consulted before other wives are taken. It may be her decision that her husband should re-marry: she may need help on the farm, or someone to cook while she is trading. If she wishes to return to her mother's house to have her baby, she may feel it her duty to find a replacement before she leaves. In these situations she may contribute to the dowry for a junior wife or even pay the whole sum. It is not uncommon to hear a woman complaining that the young wife for whom she has paid will give her neither respect nor obedience.

A junior wife may be expected to prostrate herself before her seniors, to get up early to grind their foodstuffs in a heavy mortar, and to fetch water whenever needed. She may be younger than the senior wife's children and may spend her adolescence as household drudge in her husband's house. She may openly refer to the senior wife as her mistress. I remember discussing in an African Ladies' Club the fate of an English woman who had become the eighth wife of an African chief. The Nigerian ladies were shocked that the white woman had permitted herself to become a junior wife, since she would have to go barefoot, or kneel before her seniors, or grind their pepper. Most of them sincerely pitied her, but one who knew the family reported that she was on good terms with her co-wives and that her status was assured by her being the secretary to the family firm. There was a general sigh of relief.

Probably the worst ordeal of the married life of the Ibibio women is the same as that of all women; the death of children. It must never for a moment be imagined that a woman becomes accustomed to this, her greatest tragedy, however easily and however often it happens, and however poor the way of life she has to offer. It remains for any woman the great sorrow from which she will never recover.

Nigerian children slip out of life so easily that they are considered to have a special partiality for the spirit-world, to which they are always trying to return. It happens frequently that a mother bears a number of children, each of which dies before the next is born, so that it seems to the distracted mother as if her baby is continually leaving her and returning to torment her by departing again. Such a baby was said to be suffering from 'Okponka' by the Ibibios, or 'Ubanje' by the Ibos, and traditionally considered as especially cruel; his case would be brought before a native doctor who would take steps to prevent the recurrence of this deplorable habit. Sometimes he suspends this unhappy cycle during the child's life by discovering a charm which the latter is supposed to have buried. When this is destroyed, the child ceases to ail and regains interest in this life. If the diviner is called in after an infant's death, he will mark the little body so that if a new child is born and is found to be similarly marked (which apparently happens), he will know it is the same cruel baby returned to plague its parents. If this happens several times, the poor corpse will be damaged in such a way,—i.e. by the breaking of legs— that his spirit will be unable to get back to his mother's house. After this he will be cast away without the correct burial so that he will not even reach the next world and cannot begin to reincarnate.

Probably the commonest form of death for children is from the convulsions resulting from the high fevers of malaria. One usual treatment for this is the oiling of the body and the giving of sedative herbs by enema. Sometimes pepper is used as a counter-irritant in eyes and nose. One of the herbs used in the enema is the succulent plant which we know as mother-in-law's tongues. Many native doctors have a high reputation for curing convulsions; I have known European-trained African doctors who will send their children to hospital for all other ailments, but will send for the 'dibia' in the case of convulsions. Expatriate doctors, however, claim that the hospitals could cure convulsions if only the parents would bring in the children early enough.

Ibibio mothers, like those in most parts of West Africa, suckle their babies for about two years and, if the child is insistent, for longer. A mother will test the goodness of her milk by expressing a little into a cup and then putting in an ant. If the ant dies, she must give the babe to someone else to suckle. Any woman of the family who is not lactating and who wishes to suckle the baby may induce lactation by rubbing her breasts with a particular herb. Even an old grandmother who has long ceased to bear children may perform this service for her daughters. African traditional mothers can thus be seen to have solutions to problems which modern 'civilised' mothers cannot solve. But they also have their own problems, unknown to urban housewives, such as how to cool down breast milk to baby's temperature, when coming in from tilling the sun-drenched fields.

It has been statistically demonstrated that African babies walk earlier than those of paler races, just as they generally mature earlier. Nevertheless, their mothers are often discontented with their prowess, and medicine to make babies 'toddle' is given them. The Ibibio remedy for making an infant toddle is as follows: Take the root and seeds of Ntuen ibok or Ntinya (pink desmodium). Grind the root, and adding three or five seeds, give as cold enema.

For many childhood ailments, the Ibibio old wives do not need the services of a native doctor. In the forest surrounding their cottages grow the trees whose bark, leaves, fruit and seeds they collect to pound and simmer. An Ibibio schoolteacher gave me the following list. Although neither she nor I knew the botanical names for most of the herbs, I include it here in case some botanist or pharmacist who knows the vernacular may supply the missing links. One cryptic term on the list, 'custos affer', may be the custard-apple, though that is hardly a botanical name.

One must also remember that these remedies are not used according to the simple instructions in column two; but also require ritual observations, without which they are not expected to be efficacious. Such rules must be observed as:

one must not greet anybody on the road while going for the herb or returning with it,

Herbs

For	Treatment	Vernacular names	Botanical names
Cuts	Apply the juice of the leaves	1 Mbritem 2 Udok Mbiet	Custos affer ?
Burns	Apply on the affected part the juice of the leaves	1 Atimense 2 Nsehe Nyah	Emilia
Bleeding	Apply the juice of	Edemerong	Aspilia, Custos affer
Stomach ache	Beat the leaves and drink after draining.	1 Isim Oyot 2 Etidot	? Bitter leaf
Fever	Squeeze the juice on to the skin. Take enema with the leaves.	Ekpong Idiongo	Emilia ?
Consti-pation	Burn the dry plantain peeling and drain for drinking, or take enema with	Ntong	Aspilia Bitter leaf
whooping cough and ordinary cough	Hold the leaf to the flame and squeeze out the liquid and drink	Nnening	?
Jaundice	Cut the bark of mango, collect African pear leaves, boil and get out the colour together with other com-pounds as——— then take enema with and bathe with the liquid	Eba Enenang Nkarika Ikot	?
Diarrhoea	Beat the leaves, add some cold water and native chalk, drain and take enema with	1 Ndidi 2 Mmong powder 3 Ifot Ebot 4 Nkubia 5 Ntan Isong	? Dissotis ? A creeping herb
Ring-worm	Rub the leaves in the hand and firmly on the ring-worm after scraping it.	1 Nkim Eyo 2 Abia Ikana	? ?
Excessive Menstrual Bleeding	Beat the leaves and take a cold enema with	Editan	?
Pile	Beat the leaves and take a cold enema with	Editia Idang Udok Mbiet	? ?
Acute diarrhoea and Dysentery	Beat the bark or the pod together with tender leaves of and take enema in cold water	Ibong Offuo	Kola ?
Making a child toddle	Grind the root of adding 3 or 5 seeds of and give a cold enema	Ntuen Ibok or Ntinya	Pink Desmodium
Decayed teeth	Boil the tender leaves of and with the liquid give the mouth a brisk whisk	Nsukakara	?

The question signs mean that the botanical names are not known.

also

one must not touch a broom the whole of that day.

Since Nigerian women are obsessionally courteous and houseproud, the difficulty of carrying out these instructions forms a convenient alibi for the failure of the cure.

Certain remedies on this list and many others I have not mentioned involve annointing or bathing the whole body. Modern medicine which has its roots in the customs of cold climates has ignored the possibilities of such practices. To cover the entire body surface with warm oil is a psychotherapy undoubtedly soothing and euphoric, and dispels anxiety and irritation. The effect of other kinds of liquid should be well worth examing.

The concept of spoiling a baby is unknown to an African mother. Expatriate mothers accustomed to leaving their infants to cry them-selves to sleep in cot or pram are highly shocking to the Africans. Nevertheless, it is not entirely from compassion that they quiet the crying child, since if neighbours or relatives hear it, they will say that the child's mother has been unfaithful to her husband during preg-nancy and that the child reproaches her, demanding a confession. Little nursemaids or older sisters are usually employed to look after babies while the mother is engaged in other duties. If there is no such person available, the baby goes everywhere on his mother's back. It is a charming and touching sight to see two Nigerian mothers meeting: first they curtsy and greet each other formally, then each turns the back to show the other her baby.

However, permissiveness ends with infancy, or as they say, when a child learns sense. The little girls who carry on one hip the heavy baby are severely disciplined and soon learn that obedience is the cardinal female virtue.

Children are nevertheless their parents' riches, and a woman will not consider herself unhappy if she has living children or grandchildren.

A child has a religious role also to his parents, since no one else can perform the burial rites which ensure them a speedy sojourn in the spirit world and a happy rebirth into an appropriate station. Never-theless this aspect of having children does not seem to bear nearly so much weight for the mother as for the father. It would appear that mothers have a greater concern for this world than the next, and also that they cherish their children more for themselves than for their function.

It is chiefly the duty of a man's eldest son to see to the correct celebration of his burial; and it is a woman's eldest son (in a poly-gamous household this is not necessarily the same person) who is expected to care for his mother in her old age. Since girls are fre-quently married off in infancy to men much their senior, it is extremely likely that most women will experience many years of widowhood. During this time they are fortunate to have a sur-viving son and thus enjoy respect and consideration in their latter days.

Traditionally, the only serious love relationship of the African man's life is that with his mother. This love-bond must be exceed-ingly strong to survive the ritual separation which usually forms an important part of a boy's initiation ceremonies at puberty. Among some primitive peoples he is expected at this time to flog his mother and all other old women of his family who have mothered him. This does not happen among the Ibibio, but there is, as with most West African tribes, a ritual spurning of the female virtues of peace and gentleness. It would appear to be a conviction among pre-literate peoples that a boy cannot turn into a man by natural development, and if left in his mother's company he might turn out to be a woman. This belief is by no means limited to Africa but would seem to have been the rule in most countries at some stage of their development. In parts of Africa, however, the segregation of the sexes into two castes is almost unique. When a young Ibibio man joins the society of adult males he becomes an apprentice member of a politico-religious underground movement, one of whose chief functions is the subjugation of women both in the home and in society.

Disguised as horrifying ancestral spirits, the society officials would periodically parade through the villages, beating non-members and killing women found outside their houses. They could also be called in to flog wives or daughters considered guilty of disrespect to their menfolk.

The origin of the West African judicial secret societies lies buried in prehistory. Although they are found among a variety of peoples stretching from the Congo to Sierra Leone, speaking different languages and having no obvious contact with each other, many of their rituals and functions are identical. It is difficult to believe that this could be a case of parallel social evolution. Since there is no great geographical separation, it would rather appear that this curious form of government originated in one place and was copied by observers on fishing and trading expeditions along the coast who considered it to be a good idea. Since the Efik-Ibibio peoples are traditionally regarded by their neighbours as the most ancient clan in Eastern Nigeria who were already there when everybody else arrived, their own legend of the beginning of this class of men's secret societies may be the true one. It is at any rate a fascinating story and may be seen as a possible key to one of the mysteries of pre-history.

The Ibibio legend runs that in the old days only women knew the secrets and mysteries of the gods, and this enabled them to enslave the men and employ them on the heaviest tasks; this was at a time when women greatly outnumbered men on the earth.

However, the time came when men increased in number and during one fighting expedition they unknowingly captured the shrine of the women's cult, containing the masks, fetishes and robes necessary for the performance of the power-giving ritual of the Great Mother of the Avenging Spirits.

Not knowing how to make use of these properties, they begged the priestesses to share with them their divine skills.

The women consulted together, the older ones being in favour of conserving their secrets, lest the men take them away from them; and the younger ones praising the loyalty of their menfolk till their elders gave in.

Unfortunately, it was as the old wives had predicted. When the secrets were revealed to the men they beheaded the old priestesses and declared that such would be the fate of all women who attempted to participate or even witness the ritual from that day forth.

This myth could be true on many levels. The part about the women outnumbering the men may have had a degree of truth at some time when wild beasts were more numerous than today, causing a rapid turnover of young hunters and a greater dependence upon the surviving women elders, who were then—as now—the agricultural mainstay of the population. All farming methods were obscured and hidden within the fertility cult of the Great Mother; even the fattening of the young maidens was part of the propitiation of the Earth Goddess, and in some places it is reported that one would be dedicated and eaten to induce fertility both of the soil and of its devotees. It was, as my modern Ibibio informant said of its more harmless development, 'wholly and solely a woman's affair'. Probably the farming together with the organization of the marketing of produce gave the women enviable power, and they were able to employ some of the young men as labourers and bodyguards just as the market mammies do to this day. And perhaps, though this is only my guess, at the centre of this economic power was the totem which was both a great source of food and a great birth symbol: the yam.

In Ashanti, where matrilineal society still obtains, the yam is planted by the women, and at harvest festival women have been known to tie these great tubers on their backs with their cloths as if they were babies. This was possibly the case once in Nigeria, before the patriarchal pastoralists were pushed from the north and infiltrated the matrilineal coastal tribes.

Perhaps many times in history, the herdsmen, hunters and warriors have envied what they thought was woman's easier conquest of the soil, and they have stolen the earth-spirit together with her avenging furies, and her greatest crop and totem. But since men are endowed with cunning as well as superior strength, they have arranged agriculture to their own advantage, continuing to allow women to scrape subsistence from the soil, while only the father of each family may harvest, hoard and eat the yam from the fields which the women have tended throughout the season. It is most cleverly arranged in West Africa that the patriarch will divide his plots of land between his womenfolk, who are then allowed to plant their crops of the inferior coco-yams, cassava, etc., between his rows of yams, so that they must inevitably hoe his crop which they are forbidden to touch. And at the yam harvest comes the great festival of the earth-goddess, now the reigning deity of the men's secret society. When her statue is carried through the villages, all women must hide for fear of flogging or decapitation by the avenging ancestral spirits, whom they know very well to be their husbands hiding within grotesque masks.

The remains of the women's own societies still exist today. The Ibibio women still automatically join 'Iban Isong', the daughters of the land, when they are circumcised and fattened. Their power is limited to a little trade-union activity against delinquent husbands; those, for example, who allow their goats to eat their wives' crops, etc., and some judicial activity among themselves. One of the following old wives' stories concerns a legal action taken by the women's society upon a notorious thief who dared to ignore their rule of banishment. The women were highly indignant that the colonial authorities punished them for carrying out their traditional code.

The daughters of the land naturally concern themselves with harvest festivals, although their major role has been monopolized by their masters. Fertility rites are invariably sexual to some degree, the reproduction of crops being seen as part of the wider pattern of nature which includes the reproduction of humanity. For this reason, the ritual activities of African women's societies was seen by some Victorian missionaries as a form of debauchery, much more disgraceful in a woman than in a man. Doubtless the stealing of the Great Earth Mother took place in European prehistory so long ago that white men have forgotten why they consider it less reprehensible for men to behave libidinously at festivals. The Rev. Robert Hamill Nassau, who was for forty years a missionary in the French Congo area at the end of the last century, felt justified in laying about him with his stick when he came upon women initiating girls into the dance routine which formed part of the women's society harvest rituals. Little did this otherwise kindly gentleman know that he was intuitively supporting the pagan practices of the men with identical and most un-Christian crudity.

To return to the men's societies, it was undoubtedly, from a short-term viewpoint, a stroke of genius on the part of whoever decided to incorporate the spirit of agriculture and creation within the spirit of tyranny and repression, and thus form an efficient and self-perpetuating government by a minority of male elders which had only to be seen to be copied, if we are to judge from the similarity of societies such as Poro, Oro, Ogboni, Ekkpe, Egbo, Ekkpo Njawhaw and countless others.

Although all free mature males were initiated as members of one of these societies, one must not imagine they achieved power immediately. On the contrary, they were at first merely removed from the power of their mothers to that of the old men, and held there by the promise that they could work their way up to a similar position by a series of payments to the society funds. But because such reasons would not, to begin with, separate the pubescent boys from an atmosphere of love and devotion at their mother's hearth, they were first made to undergo an agonizing brainwashing at the hands of their elders. Often they were forced to perform some shameful act for which they would forever feel collective guilt, and at the same time they were rewarded by congratulations of the admired hunters and warriors in having achieved manhood. Usually this was combined with a hoax of a terrifying nature or a painful flogging and test of endurance, which in later years they would inflict on their juniors.

Although initiation ceremonies inevitably concern themselves with the selection of warriors, this normally coincides with the weeding out of youths of an ambitious or truculent nature. Adolescents showing signs of undesirable scepticism or independence of spirit will often be found to have suffered a fatal accident during these rituals. The accepted view of the initiation ordeals as a passage into 'manhood' is typical of the naivete permeating contemporary social theory, and might be improved by a corrective glance at the writings of the classical American anthropologist Nathan Miller, who has astutely demonstrated the reactionary nature of an institution designed to reduce the rebellious young to a state of 'cringing conformity'.

The 'warfare of the generations' signifies not only the mutual hostility of the weakening elders and the ambitious young, but also the conflict between a conservative timidity and new solutions and exploratory projects. Initiation into an elder-controlled society is thus an institution of self-perpetuating stagnation. Tribal societies practising such rituals can be seen not as 'primitive', but rather as the reverse, namely gerontocracies perpetually arrested in the spirit of old age.

The factor of a 'cold sex-war' which is a serious aspect of the activities of the West African secret-societies is perhaps equally disastrous to social development. Unlike the male initiate, the female remains throughout her life in a sub-culture or sexual-apartheid. Sir Arthur Keith, in his *New Theory of Human Evolution*, writes 'A tribe with one part free and another enslaved is no longer a single unit with a common spirit and a common destiny; it is then a twofold body with a twofold morality, and a doubtful destiny.'

He describes this as a way in which the human species has 'clogged its evolutionary machinery'; and although he is speaking of slavery as such, his diagnosis might equally well be applied to the sexual segregation enforced by the African gerontocracies through their organ of the secret-society.

In traditional Nigeria, the sex-war was of course a conflict in which one participant had apparently long since been defeated on all except what might be described as the nursery-front. The chief power left to women was that made possible by the love of their sons, so this must every generation be redestroyed by the bogus ancestral spirits through the brainwashing of the boys. In the following stories we read of one woman who reckoned her age by the date when one poor victim died because she was caught in the open street by the men's society during one of its festivals; and the old men, when questioned about the year, casually say that so many women died that way in those days that they are unable to date it.

But the nature of women is such that we may read in another story of a woman who was proud to purchase for her son an office in this same society.

It is very sad to reflect that during the conflict between the Federal Government of Nigeria and the seceding Eastern Region of Biafra, the secret-societies have resorted to their original function of intimidating women in the main streets of the capital cities. During the years of peace following Independence, African judges attempted to stamp out the remains of these activities when they still took place in remote villages by transforming them into a kind of carnival, and instructing the masked performers not to wound with their machets any creatures other than dogs or goats. Nevertheless, a system so beneficial to the toughest section of the population is difficult to remove.

The Ibibio women whose lives make up this book have still cowered in terror behind the insecure doors of their houses, when the bell rings to mark the coming of the 'Masquerade', as this pogrom has been euphemistically translated. Their educated daughters, even though travelled overseas, will often refuse to sit in the room of an expatriate who hangs a ritual mask for decoration on his wall.

Unfortunately, it is quite possible to speculate that the obscurantism and atmosphere of terror which surround the fertility cult were in the first place the invention of the women to defend their agricultural secrets from the stronger sex. However, when the tables were turned, the men reinforced the panic-creating set-up with physical violence, greatly multiplying its effect and establishing a most unfortunate psychological 'feed-back' system. For to terrify the mother is to learn terror at the mother's knee. As psychologists have learned, one of the greatest causes of mental unbalance is a childhood environment of fear, and the mother is the child's environment.

To survive generations of terrorism, the African woman has

evolved an unusual degree of stoicism, cheerfulness and endurance, which fortunately she can convey to her children. But every generation until recently was re-taught a conglomeration of imaginary fears, and spiritually the boy fared worse than the girl, since, in addition to fear, he was taught deviousness and hypocrisy and the destruction of the bonds of love.

Since they are programmed into the mammalian psyche, the bonds of love cannot be destroyed without destroying the species. The desire to love can hardly be driven out of the human female, and an answering echo of love can never be entirely stamped out of her sons, although they may be filled with a stultifying inner conflict.

You will hear little in these stories about 'Masquerade', partly because the Missions had already drawn the teeth from this monstrous custom, and partly because it is for women a forbidden subject and a nightmare which they prefer to forget. The system, however, is reflected in the fact that the women hardly ever emerge as individuals until they become members of their sons' households. The contemptuous and truculent manner which a man was traditionally expected to bear towards his wife is reflected in the descriptions of the happily married women. These invariably describe their marriage in the terms of another relationship. 'He was like a father to me', or 'We were like brother and sister', or 'He treated me as his mother'.

Some mention is made by these old wives of the customs in their mothers' generation for widows to undergo lengthy ordeals and incarcerations. This often appalling treatment, which the more naïve anthropologists interpreted as 'mourning', seems to demonstrate another strategy of the sex-war on the part of the patriarchy, namely a technique for discouraging husband-poisoning. Whether the latter existed or not (and Mary Kingsley thought it so rife as to justify the excesses of the Egpo), the fact that it was assumed to be probable, indicates a deplorably poor marital bond.

At some point in West African history, a tribal Machiavelli invented a trial for widows consisting of diving under their husband's canoe, whereby the wife who was too decrepit to avoid jogging the craft was considered to be the poisoner, and therefore executed. Since the remaining athletes might be expected to be satisfactory farm-hands, the system was without doubt beneficial to the husband's brother who inherited them.

For a comfortable old age, the Ibibio woman is dependent upon her daughters-in-law, and it would appear that she has rarely cause for complaint. Since they come often as mere infants into her house they are more like adopted daughters, and they have in any case been trained in filial duties and obedience almost from babyhood. The relationship between mother-in-law and daughter-in-law is one of the tightest bonds in the Nigerian family, and often causes a severe cultural shock to foreign girls who marry Nigerian students abroad before joining their families. It is also a great cause of fear in the hearts of the African mothers who send their sons overseas that they will marry expatriate women who turn out mothers from their rightful place at the head of their son's household.

Unless prevented by dutiful children, the Ibibio old wife will continue to farm and trade into old age, for on this depends her self-respect and her ability to contribute to her family's progress. She may have more time for social life, and indeed will join her age-group in dance festivals almost to the end. In old age she may even have won the respect and admiration of her husband, and she will certainly be the adviser of her sons and daughters, and be in demand as a story-teller to her grandchildren.

The old women who tell the stories in this book have broken to some extent with traditional religious observances and are mostly partial members of some church women's society. By becoming practising Christians, they once more put themselves under the leadership of a male figure-head, which critics of colonial rule have described as a retrogressive step in female emancipation. This I believe to be a hypocritical criticism and part of the false flattery of those who wish to inherit the power without the responsibility of the departing colonials. Any student of African history will realize how little the women had to lose by departing from tradition, though the same cannot be said of the men.

Many traditional religious practices have been secularized and preserved. Most Missions became accustomed to the enthralling music and dancing which had first been condemned. It was my pleasure to witness, at the opening of the Council of Social Sciences at Port Harcourt, a bishop blessing the female dancers, whose pelvic rocking would have brought blushes to the cheeks of earlier travellers.

Nowadays, tribal unions exist among townswomen, to preserve their link with their villages. Before I left Nigeria, I heard that the Ibibio women's union in Port Harcourt had contributed the cost of sending home one of their members who had been abandoned by her husband and did not feel able to face the 'free' life of the city.

Charitable organizations begun by the wives of expatriate officials and workers, are now almost entirely taken over by African professional wives who, being supplied with domestic help to a degree which any European or American would envy, have ample leisure time to fill with good works.

The Nigerian Y.W.C.A. is a splendid example of the organization and unity of the mature professional and business women, many of whose mothers have led lives similar to those in this book. They devote themselves to the establishment of nursery schools, girls' hostels, literacy classes for grown women and the general dissemination of culture. Moreover, by international standards, they form a gathering of extraordinary glamour in their immaculate and scintillating costumes, their splendid bearing, beaming faces and air of well-being. They revel in femininity; their robes are more becoming to the pregnant woman than the slim; they radiate power.

The power of the African woman whether modern or traditional is indeed paradoxical. Taken item by item, the situations in which she is exploited or subjugated add up to something indistinguishable from slavery. She enters her husband's house as a kitchen-maid; though enabled to farm for profit, she will never have property rights. If dismissed, she will not have custody of her children. When widowed, she does not inherit; on the contrary, she is inherited. How then has she seemed so obviously powerful to expatriate observers? Anthropologist Evans Pritchard has dismissed contemptuously attempts to sympathize with her seemingly wretched status. African writers themselves are at their most ecstatic when praising a charismatic village matron or a 'Jagwa-full' city hostess.

Perhaps it is partly because the sullen and ferocious African patriarchy has never fully been established; has never felt sufficiently secure as to become a benevolent paternalism. The legends of the age of women's rule are, after all, still part of spoken tradition, and the secret-society of the men still requires in the last resort an ancient hag to complete its ritual.

Nigerian prehistory becomes daily less accessible. If the secret of the African woman's paradoxical power lies in the past, evidence is limited and the act of detection highly speculative, depending entirely upon the harmony and coherence of a few artifacts, some historical documents of an unscientific nature, the researches of a few dedicated scholars at the early part of the twentieth century, a mass of unsifted modern urban sociology and the application of an almost untried new behavioural science, ethology.

However objectively one views the ambiguity of the present female status, it is almost impossible to avoid some acceptance of a prehistoric matriarchy.

I myself have made the most strenuous effort to avoid crossing the path of the poet Robert Graves, who has pursued the Great White Mother Goddess around the Mediterranean and into many other quarters of the globe. However, since he has traced her into Ghana, where apparently she rules in her triple aspect as moon-goddess, it is not surprising that I have finally been unable to avoid her in Old Calabar, carried upon the head of an Ibibio maiden of the Iban Isong, the daughters of the Earth-mother. White she certainly was, if by white we mean Caucasian; that is to say, her face was shocking-pink, her hair black and to her shoulders. Her costume was totally unfamiliar unless that of a Hungarian gypsy, and in her upraised and grossly elongated arms she held the giant python.

It is difficult to imagine how and from whence such a figure came to be used in a rural African cult. Apart from the forshortening of the legs and elongation of the arms, she is totally un-African. The face might be that of an Italian madonna, but no madonna wore a plain white bandeau over long and streaming hair. No saintly figurine brought by the Portuguese catholics would wear this gaudy brazen little dress; and where outside of Eden is the snake to be found in Christianity?

Let us add another class of unaccountable artifacts; namely the fortified and castellated towns identical to those of prehistoric Crete, but modelled in the typical compressed earth of West Africa, which were found by Sir Harry Johnston in Adamana in the hinterland of the Cameroons, then pass without comment to the legends.

I need not repeat the story of how the warriors stole the women's cult of Eka Ekkpo, the Mother of Avenging Spirits. Another version of the story is as follows; the first Egbo was found by some women of the Cameroons (from where the Efik-Ibibio peoples are said to originate) when they went down to fish in the river. The image was brought by water by a divine woman who had come down to earth to teach the secrets of her cult to her human sisters. After learning the mysteries the women bore the image in triumph to their town, where they built a house in which to shelter it and practise the rites of the cult. After a while the men noticed the importance of the new institution and persuaded the women to admit them to its mysteries. No sooner had they succeeded in learning these than they rose and slew all those to whom the secret had first been revealed, and made a law that for the future only men might become members of the society or be permitted to witness the rites.

Egbo is a colloqualized version of the name of the Earth-mother goddess, and it would seem beyond dispute that what the foreign priestess taught the fisher-woman was a fertility cult, i.e. either an agricultural technique or simply agriculture itself, which might have been unknown to this hunting and fishing society. We are then left to speculate as to the nature of the mystery which required the killing of its custodians. Did the 'divine woman' bring the seeds of food crops, so few of which are known to be indigenous to tropical Africa? Or was it by any chance the whole paraphernalia of festivity and sacrifice which surrounds the cult of the 'White Goddess' in Eastern Mediterranean lands?

Let us look now at the loopholes in the present patriarchiate; at the small remnants of women's power which yet carry such emotional force against all reason.

In each of the sadly courageous little autobiographies which make up this book, there is one such element.

In the story of 'The Oldest Inhabitant' we find the total astonishment of this woman that in her official capacity she was not permitted power of life or death over a thief condemned by her Society. Yet, to all intents and purposes, Ebere is a dancing club with no more function than entertainment at village celebrations. To what extent is it still accepted as the judicial society of former days?

Evidence of the acceptance of the priestly function of women is clearly demonstrated in 'The Reluctant Sorceress'. The father of this remarkable person is described by her as an occultist, which can only be taken to mean a priest of the dis-established religion, since he was a nineteenth-century village Ibibio and not a modern urban occultist who could simply be a merchant of charms from Bombay. Since despite all his sons, he insisted that his cloak should fall upon the shoulders of his daughter, and since he was supported in this decision by his sons, it is just possible to assume that his type of 'prayer-house' was one normally run by a woman. When the inner conflict of the woman, which produces such classical symptoms, is finally resolved by her acceptance of her vocation, she immediately comes into her own and demonstrates that she is by no means the simple peasant, by choosing a name for her cult quite acceptable to the local Mission, while bearing a suspicious resemblance to one of the titles of the Ibibio fertility goddess Eke Isu Ma, Goddess of the Face of Love; surely one of the most beautiful of all divine names. I myself assumed that the Holy Face was a Christian institution until my interpreter commented that the white powder with which the priestess covered herself and the five rings on her left hand were the way her deity wished her to dress.

It is also significant that no sooner had the priestess accepted her vocation than she received the active support of the women of her age-grade. Tradition dies hard.

The priestly function of women is accepted to a degree quite inconsistent with their apparent low status. In the story of 'The Slave's Daughter', the mission-trained wife converts her husband to Christianity when she 'put him to light of the glories that one could rightly own in the education of one's children'. He allowed her to convince him to the extent of 'putting away earthly things'. (He entered the Methodist Mission and reaped full benefit by 'counting changes of clothing besides living and dying in a pan-roofed house'.)

Women described as witches were not always mere scapegoats. In the story of 'The Witch's Great-Grand-Daughter' the head of the witch, who must indeed have been powerful as she died a natural death, was purchased for its intrinsic potentiality to enhance a local shrine.

The accepted judicial function of women is illustrated in the story of 'The Blind Man's Wife' by the description of this woman's first mother-in-law who intervened to ensure just treatment of her daughters-in-law by her son; and also in 'The Travelled Woman' where an outside woman friend would be called in to settle marital quarrels.

It is usual for women to arrange marriages for their sons in West Africa, and quite common for them to arrange marriages for their husbands, but in the story of 'A Reprieved Man's Daughter', the narrator tells of her marriage being arranged by a daughter of her intended husband, whom one would normally expect to be a person of very low status indeed.

The ambiguity of female status in polygamous households is demonstrated in the autobiography of 'The Lady Member of Ekpo'.

In this story, one is surprised to find that a husband of twenty-one wives can suffer from neglect. The passage is well worth quoting:

> Jealousy was always the order of the day, especially during
> the farming season. Some of my co-wives often accused my
> husband of failing to give them a better farm—that is, a more
> fertile. Cases like this created much jealousy among us, and with
> this many of us usually stayed many months without saying
> hello to one another. During these periods, my late husband
> usually suffered because those wives who feel that my husband
> had cheated them will overlook my husband and all services will
> have a breakdown until my husband must call outsiders to come
> in for settlement. During that time, the unhappy wives will not
> mind whether my husband eats or not, but all they know is to
> cook their food and eat with their children so that my husband
> might repent when it gets to such season the following year.

Many old wives declare themselves to be in favour of a polygamous household, but the wife of that unfortunate husband is its strongest supporter. As the title of her story suggests, she is one of those rare women to become a member of what is now considered an exclusively male society. But the most significant fact that emerges from this tale is that *the women* bestowed this honour upon her.

As a final piece of evidence of the unexpected power of woman in the rigidly patriarchal Ibibio culture, I should like to quote some words from an 'old wife' who was adopted into the clan, and rose to the status of uncrowned queen of Okoyong, though many knew her simply as 'Ma'. This woman, of a different ethny, and another cult, came to the area accompanied only by her domestic retinue, to teach her beliefs much in the manner of the 'divine woman' of the earlier legend. She was a person of scrupulous honesty and in communications to her distant people makes no grandiose claims of religious conversion. Therefore I think we may accept as truth her statements concerning the surprising ease by which she found her leadership accepted and her secular standards adopted. She wrote

> Of results as affecting the condition and conduct of our people
> generally, it is more easy to speak. Raiding, plundering, the
> stealing of slaves, have almost entirely ceased. Any person from
> any place can come now for trade or pleasure, and stay wherever
> they choose, their persons and property being as safe as in

Calabar. For fully a year we have heard of nothing like violence from even the most backward of our people. They have thanked me for restraining them in the past, and begged me to be their consul, as they neither wished black man nor white man to be their king. It would be impossible, apart from a belief in God's particular and personal providence in answer to prayer, to account for the ready obedience and submission to our judgment which was accorded to us. It seemed sometimes to be almost miraculous that hordes of armed drunken, passion-swayed men should give heed and chivalrous homage to a woman, and one who had neither wealth nor outward display of any kind to produce the slighest sentiment in her favour. But such was the case, and we do not recollect one instance of insubordination.

This royal passage was written by one whose training in leadership had been the care of a family of literally starving siblings in a northern slum, but who slipped into the role of female chieftainship as a hand into a glove. Even if we take into account 'God's particular and personal providence', it would seem highly likely that the role was not an unknown or unacceptable one among these people. Mary Slessor's guiding passions of the saving of life and the raising up of women, together with her ready acceptance of traditional ritual not actually conflicting with her sensible and pragmatic view of Christianity, seem to me to have found an echo from an earlier age in the people who could so easily have destroyed her. The white priestess who sat in judgment while swearing witnesses by Mbiam may in effect have had the protection of more deities than the One she officially served.

I cannot refrain from quoting another example of the Ibibio's acceptance of this diminutive queen. The occasion was during her campaign against drunkenness when she confiscated a consignment of gin. Surrounded by a host of eager and thirsty warriors, she removed her garments and covered the crates beneath its royal tabu. The grumbling army allowed themselves to be consoled with a tot each, and then dispersed peacefully.

It is possible that not merely a matrilineal past—such as I have earlier recounted many examples—is demonstrable from this evidence, but that the echoes of true matriarchy are still resounding in the ears of the many kings of this rainy country.

The situation of matriarchy, involving not only guidance but government of the physically strong by the weak, is by its nature so paradoxical that historians and sociologist engaged in the study of militarism and politics have been tempted to deny its possibility.

Indeed if one accepts the principle that physical force is necessary for power, it seems unlikely that any regime closer to matriarchy than one of matrilineal descent has been viable, and that the latter has always had as its leader not the mother of the clan but her brother.

Nevertheless, archaeologists have postulated a period of pure matriarchy, and support their theories with the evidence of prehistoric art and legend inherited from pre-literacy.

Most cultures can be traced back to matrilineal clans taking their names from a female ancestor, and a parallel origin can be found for even the most male-centred religions, involving an earth-moon mother and her priestesses. A goddess-oriented culture seems often to have persisted into a civilization where men undoubtedly held power, such as in ancient Crete; but this precarious situation has inevitably fallen as a result of internal or external pressure from patriarchal peoples bringing the male gods of fire, war, thunder and technology.

Periods of sex-war—by no means as comical as the name suggests —when patrilineal and matrilineal factions dwelt together under a system of disharmonious double-descent may be deduced from the Homeric epics, and a dramatic summary of the patriarchal takeover is in fact the whole theme of the Orestian Trilogy, where the furies, the matriarchal judicial spirits who avenge wrongs within the maternal clan, are eventually demoted to a minor domestic role by the god Apollo; and the human, Orestes, who has murdered his mother, is judged by patrilineal standards to be comparatively blameless, since by the new patriarchal law, his family is that of his father whom he avenged, and his kinship with his mother is insignificant to the point of non-existence. His mother, Clytemnestra, had justified her killing of her husband Agamemnon by the standards of the old matrilineal code, since she was avenging children of her household, to which her husband did not fully belong.

The significance of this traumatic period of social evolution is convincingly demonstrated by the American sociologist Joan Rockwell, in her valuable work *Fact in Fiction*, in which she diagnoses the high status of some early women, from evidence in the Icelandic sagas and the Mediterranean epics.

The much more accessible African pre-literate cultures show

remarkable parallels with those of the Homeric epics; and other parts of the world still neglected by civilization seem to attest to the universality of the passage from female to male authority.

Among the primitive Georgians, the patriarchal takeover is strikingly recorded by the paternal adoption of the very name of Mamma—the onomatopoeic and universal title bestowed on the human female by the first utterance of her infant. This situation is as significant of the belief in maternal supernatural powers as is the 'couvade', where the father imitates in every superficial detail the routine and ritual of his wife's parturient condition, thus taking upon himself what he imagines to be her source of power. His mistake is to see the maternal state as primarily a power-situation, whereas power is its secondary attribute, deriving firstly from the eradicable 'imprinting' of the mother upon the mind of her infant during his first years, and secondly, from the family's faith in the primary maternal qualities of altruistic dedication and responsibility.

Much of West African traditional family life is still at the stage following the patriarchal takeover when peace is insecurely maintained by the segregation of the sexes almost into two nations, and the administering of a love-potion by a wife to her husband is regarded as a capital offence.

The 'woman's world' preserves its underground, and at times of crisis such as the threat of female taxation, or the raising of school-fees, demonstrates organization and preparedness. An African observer of the first Aba Riots of 1929–30 describes his panic when he found women massing in the villages *without children*. (An imbecilic French novelist demonstrated his ignorance recently by describing African women rioters 'brandishing' their infants.)

One riot which was triggered off by a false rumour of taxation, was considered to cover an area of ninety miles across. It converged on the District Office and caused the death of several colonial officers before the misunderstanding was cleared. A later riot was aimed at the newly created African politicians who had found themselves forced to abolish free primary education. An army of country women were brought into the town by their willing but non-combatant menfolk on the front of bicycles and in lorry-loads, and were thought at first to be men in disguise. The cement houses of the unsatisfactory delegates were attacked with machets by the irate village matrons and many razed to the ground.

In one of the last newspapers to reach me from beleaguered Biafra, a local Boadicea was reported to be haranging her compatriots declaring that Biafran women were prepared to defend their country alone. Indeed, sexual competition in defence can be seen in the Biafran posters, one of which shows a plump lady demolishing an enemy with a club, and exhorts the men to leave this type of warfare to the women and use manlier methods.

Warfare of any kind, whether the carnage which accompanies civilization, or the class-war, or even the sex-war, may be viewed either as symptomatic of an irrepressible instinct of aggression or as the inevitable consequences of unbearable conditions of stress. The land-saturation which curtailed the peaceful agricultural life of the prehistoric Ibibio, setting village against village and sex against sex; and the present bitter struggle for the vital mineral resources necessary to huge populations, are the roots of a violence which seems to me to be universally unwelcome to the humble individual, and to afford few instinctual satisfactions.

The stories of the old Ibibio wives demonstrate one thing with certainty, that however stressful the social framework, even when it demands ritual hostility within the very heart of the family, and covers the springs of life with a smokescreen of bitter obscurantism, so that a majority of outsiders have felt justified in speaking of a 'heart of darkness', and even modern ethnographers can conceive of an entity describable as the 'savage mind', within this environment there persists a simple continuity of responsible and affectionate vigilance, a firm bond of warmth and love stretching from a forgotten past and maintaining its immaculate integrity in the face of cruel custom.

The quality in all mothers which I have described elsewhere as the 'messianic drive', is found without exception in these women, who reach out to grasp the education and betterment of their children.

So many of these old grandmothers whose lives seem devoid of any spiritual nourishment, describe themselves as the most fortunate of women, because of the survival of a pitiful minority of their offspring.

The innocent glory of the young girls' parade in the market-place after fattening, blissfully upraised upon the shoulders of the strong young men, sheds its radiance over a life of seeming drudgery. And even this apparent drudgery of tropical farming is looked upon as a great compensation in an otherwise impoverished life.

And how many of the fathers in these stories live and die respected and loved by their great families, regardless of the ferocious and love-rejecting indoctrination of their adolescence; and end their days dispensing wisdom as worthily as the patriarchs of the Old Testament, whose example has been the model for western civilization throughout the centuries.

The reluctant sorceress

I am a native of Obio Etoi, married at Aka Offar, a village about two miles from Uyo. I cannot know exactly my age because when I was born there was no birth records and secondly my parents were pure illiterates.

I was given to marriage at the time I was able to wear only a yard of cloth. I had not yet big breasts but I married as it was then the custom to give out girls for marriage at early age. I have not married more than once. In our days, women were made to marry only one husband. A woman was not allowed to divorce her husband if even she was maltreated except she had an exceptional cause before that could be allowed as it was in my own case. Yes, my husband is still living, but I am no longer under his own control due to the job I am now partaking. I started life with him as a wife when I was very young.

My father was an occultist who helped many lives around the area then. As a first daughter to my father, before he died, he said that I would be the person to carry on with what activities he would leave behind. I never took what he said seriously but rather I considered it as an old man's opinion. To my greatest surprise, two or three years after his death, strange things started to happen one after the other. The first strange thing that happened contrary to my expectation was that my physical outlook got changed as if I had been put into the fattening house. I was fat in so much that people like my husband and other relatives started fearing me. Nobody agreed sharing anything in common with me because I was fearful to look at. Investigations started from all sources to find out what might have been the cause of such a rapid fatness. All efforts and sacrifices made, were all mere waste of time, and instead of seeing any good improvements, I became fatter, yellow and fearful. After so much effort people starting getting fed up and waited to see what would be the outcome of such unnecessary fatness especially to a person whose parents were slender including the children.

The fatness lasted seven months and after that I gradually grew thinner, till I attained my normal form again. Nobody knew how the thinness took effect nor was anything made again when all attempts resulted in failure when the thing newly started. After I had grown thin, the whole family were directed to one of the best native doctors to know what had been the cause of such fatness. Here was the time that it was revealed that I should continue with my father's handwork immediately, if not something more serious would again happen in less than seven days from the day the thinness occurred.

When this report came to me I hardly believed it as I thought such a thing couldn't cause such a disgraceful fatness. When I started saying this, my relatives were against the idea but I strongly confirmed to them that mere talking could not have any effect on me especially as my father was so much interested in me. Seven days had not yet expired when I got missed* in my husband's house, and this time I became useless and I could hardly distinguish any good thing from the bad one.

Devil spirits drove me out of the house into a thick forest for one year and nobody was able to see me, nor did my husband or any of my relatives know my whereabouts, nor did all the sacrifices made lead to my discovery. I became a slave to evil spirits that controlled me entirely and I was also made to become dumb. My husband and relatives wasted all their money to know my whereabouts but nothing was heard of me.

When I had been in the forest for one year, my senior brother one day met with my father in a dream and he was told of the whole thing that occurred to me. There my father told the son that all that they saw happened as a result of my stubbornness and that if he could help them know my whereabouts he should advise me to do the job he told me; if not, so he would die. He told my brother all the sacrifices to be made before he parted and my brother woke.

After all the sacrifices were performed, in one of the biggest forests in Aka Offar, my eyes were made to see my many relatives who came to witness the sacrifice. There I called my brother behind a big mahogany tree; they all shouted and were frightened, but when they recognized me behind a mahogany tree they were so astonished, so

* Disappeared from.

terrified, so overjoyed, for heaven's sake how came you here? After everything had been done they went away with me down to my home.

Though people were happy at seeing me back many of them were still fearing me because they thought my senses were not so correct as before. Of course, the fear lasted for only a very short time and people started being familiar with me once more. My relatives did everything for me as my father directed my brother in the dream and I was made to start up the job in full swing. Those who had previous experience of the job, told me to divorce my husband so that my late father might not get me punished for having two masters at a time. I refused the idea at first but I was later made to understand that if I still continued with my husband, the worst would come to me. This finally made me to divorce my husband and stay unmarried till this present time.

My husband was then a smuggler, but now he does nothing because he has no money and he is not very active again. I was then the only wife of the man, but when I got missed, he married two other women who are still with him now.

I lived in my parents' house when I was not yet married, but later I stayed with my husband till the time the incident occurred and finally I was back to my father's compound where I built my own house for my business. I don't like any place other than where I am living because it was the wish of my husband, father and relatives that I should stay here. Nothing happened to me again after the fulfilment of my father's words and I am really happy that this incident happened after I had already got children.

When I married my husband, I started my life as a farmer until when my father died, when I automatically put a stop to it due to what happened to me after his death. Since I took up this job, I have not done any other thing than this.

I gave birth to six children in my husband's house and four died leaving two boys. They have both married with eight children totally. My first son is a trader with six children while the brother is a fisherman with two children.

The happiest time in my life was when my father died. The reason why I consider that time a happy one was because my father died when all his children were at home. It was indeed a glorious death and we actually gave him the last honour from the day he died till the day of the burial. We arranged his burial in the way that pleased nearly everybody. His burial awarded us many good names due to how it was planned just for his own honour. That is why I thought it was the happiest time for me because we showed people that our father had dutiful children.

When my people discovered me from the forest where I was hidden by evil spirits, I was indeed ashamed and unhappy when I realized what had actually happened to me. When I remembered as I was found naked behind a mahogany tree like a mad woman, I was very unhappy and ashamed within myself. This was the most unhappy time I ever experienced.

The most interesting thing that ever happened to me was when I was blessed and appointed the first woman 'prophetised'* under the Holy Face in the whole of this area. This happened as a result of my good job since I carried on my father's job. My father was not working under the Holy Face, rather he established a certain prayer house where people usually gathered to sing and pray for my father's long life. Goats, chickens, and other eatable things were often presented to people on such days to encourage many people coming in. When women of my age saw all various healing and wonders I had been performing they suggested that I should combine with them together, so that they might assist in drawing the attention of many people. I did as they said and when sufficient money was collected, we established the society as a church and nicknamed it 'Holy Face'. Of course this took effect when we started seeing that people were more civilized and were no longer interested in superstition. This was how the Holy Face came to this area. Nearly all the Holy Faces in Offar originated from my compound. My own healing is incomparable to any other and that has been the reason why more people rush in than to any other one.

All members of my family are kind to me because I am the only well-to-do person in the family who looks after my brother's children as others are not financially strong. Since I started this job I have helped them as much as I can even in educating their children. Of course, they are the people showing me the best way that my money should be spent as none of my children were educated.

In my position I am not expected to be going out but those coming to me are those needing my assistance. Some of them have been helping me in domestic affairs and also in farm work. I use them as my daughters as I am more or less a mother to them. I help them in

* Established as a prophetess.

buying them dresses, caring for them and also helping their parents in paying their school fees.

I am not afraid to say my mother was very greedy simply because she did not know God. She never spent her money for any other person other than her own children.

I have led a plain and simple life. Even though my own children were born during the time that people knew very little about the value of education, and none of them were trained, but yet I have had the love to see that all of them were brought up in the way that would benefit them in the future.

If anybody offends me I always pardon and forget about whatever offence the person committed, but my mother always retaliated anybody who offended her. She knew nothing about God and she had never wanted anybody to tell her anything in connection with God. She never wanted to take corrections because she thought that whatever she did was the best. Of course she did all that to suit with the condition of life at that time.

Life these days is more simple and better than the days when I was young. If life were as plain and simple as this when I was young, at least one of my children could have been trained, and they could not have suffered as they do now. In those days, people lived a primitive and backward life and little was known about the value of education. People were selfish and never minded the progress and well-being of their fellow men.

Commentary

In Ibibioland, as is demonstrated by this story, fatness is not in itself considered a mark of beauty. 'Unofficial' fatness, outside the fattening-house, is obviously considered a disgrace. This adds support to the theory that official fattening has as its purpose something other than aesthetics, and may well be a demonstration of fertility or 'pseudo-fertility'.

We have also a case of 'pseudo-Christianity' in this story, whereby the traditional priestess endows her cult with a veneer of respectability, to evade conflict with the Missions. Ambiguous cults of this nature are frequently found in the suburbs of modern Nigerian towns, and quite closely resemble certain American Negro patterns of worship. They are however curiously distinct from the mediumistic 'possession' cults found in the ex-French West Indies and in parts of Africa previously colonized by Catholic countries. The lady who tells this story regrets her temporary possession by spirits, and makes no attempt to carry it with her into her religious-medical practice. Why Protestant-colonized countries should favour prophetic cults, and Catholic-colonized countries mediumistic ones I have not yet discovered, though it may be connected with an interpretation of saints as ancestral spirits.

Of psychological and theological interest is the conviction found here that divorce was essential because of religious vocation.

The home daughter

I am a native of Igvitaly, a village about seven miles from Port Harcourt township. I was brought to this town (Uyo) by one of my townsmen who was then a bar master. The man had been importing palm wine from Ikot Ekpene and I was the woman in charge of the palm wine and then other young ladies helped in selling the wine to the men coming in to drink.

I am almost fifty years of age. You can even see this from my appearance. One good thing I see is that when a woman stays in the town her life differs from the village she was in.

I am the first daughter of my father and it was our custom that all first daughters must remain unmarried, rather they must give themselves to any man who loves them. As many children as the woman can get, she leaves to her own father who takes good care of them as his real children. I lived in my father's compound since I was born until the time I grew old and could not deliver children any longer. My father always permitted me to move to anywhere on condition that I bring back money to him.

I have lived in many places around my village. I have also experienced more town life than most of my junior sisters who were married. This happened because I was given liberty of doing anything I liked. I lived with one of my friends at Ekele. Though Ekele was then as bushy as my village was, I enjoyed it more than my village because they welcomed me well as a stranger. During that time, though our Ikwere headquarters was not then developed, but it was the nearest township to us and we experienced a bit of town life there.

I like township life more than village life because no matter how old or ugly one is, one is able to see many new people coming to settle there, and life would not be so difficult because one must also come across those of the same group with him.

I would not describe my life as a happy one because of this strong custom that ruled me. Though it was then our custom for first daughters to stay unmarried yet there is no peace within their minds because anybody, no matter whether they liked them or not, must approach them for friendship. My children all died and I had no one to help me financially. If my children were alive perhaps by now I should have been with them. During farming season if one does not buy her own land for farming it means that she will not farm because the father would not give her any. Except one has a mother, perhaps she may be given a small portion of land by her. In those days people thought that if first daughters were given any consideration on this, there would be some who would prefer to depend on their fathers instead of worrying themselves with men. If our forefathers had allowed our fathers to give first daughters lands to farm, it meant many of us could have refused the idea of being free because we knew that, whether we had people outside or not, we could still have what to eat.

When I was at home, I always bought some land to farm with. In the absence of that, I did some small trading to enable me to earn a living.

I had three daughters but all died leaving me with four of their children. The four children were my second daughter's children and they are now staying with their father. My first and third daughters died when they were very small.

When I was a young lady, life was sweet and enjoyable. But when I started growing older I saw myself a different person entirely. In those days, I had sufficient money to satisfy my wants. Even though I was living a primitive life, I enjoyed it because I had everything I needed freely. That was the only time I experienced a happy time in life.

My unhappy days started when I started growing older. Some of my age mates depend on their children, but I have not got anybody to depend on. If even one of my children were alive, things could not have been what they are now with me. As my children had all died, at least I should have sisters and brothers to take care of me, yet there is none of these people. My unhappiness started when these people started dying one after the other. If any of these people were alive, I could not have stayed outside my village, particularly this time that I am growing older to work for my daily bread. The fellow who brought me to this town was a husband to one of my late sisters.

When he saw how bad my condition was, he sympathized with me as if I were his mother.

The most exciting thing that happened to me was during the time of my circumcision. In Ikwere, when a girl is about to have the first child, she must first of all be circumcised. As a first daughter, they took me away from my father's compound to a neighbouring compound so that both my mother and father had not the liberty of seeing me, until they were permitted to do so. It was the custom that before any parents saw their daughter, certain traditional rites must be observed and such parents must also be in readiness to equip their daughters' houses with utensils. Any parents failing to do that, were often ordered to stay away from where the circumcised girls were until such a time they felt they could afford to do according to the custom before their daughters were released to them. Though my parents were poor, they did more than what some richest parents did to their daughters. They also gave me some money to start trading at my convenient time.

Though I am not married, I feel it would be a bad thing for a woman when the husband has more than one wife. There would be a lot of discriminations between children of the other co-wives. Anything that could be sufficient for one wife would be shared for many. There would be a lot of misunderstanding and jealousy. Other co-wives might feel that their husband does not love them equally and thereby death can occur unexpectedly. Those are some of the reasons why I suggest that it would be a bad thing for a woman if the husband has more than one wife.

My grandfather was the kindest person to me, but since he died there is nobody as good as that again to me.

I have many friends outside my family but some of them were not reliable, therefore I had to refriend. Some of them have been giving me financial help. In time of trouble some of them usually help me to see that nobody finds me guilty when I am at right. I usually help them in their need, provided it is within my power to do it.

My mother was shy in doing anything, especially as she was born into a primitive society. She had never gone out to any distant place other than her village. She did everything with fear. She thought nobody could earn a living except he or she was a wealthy trader who went to market carrying a small market basket on her head, and could count her manillas up to an astonishing number of bunches. Though I am an illiterate as my mother was, yet my life has got many good changes due to my raised standard of life. The west coast English I can now speak is the benefit I had derived from visiting some strange places outside my village. My mother usually tied some clothes around her waist bare bodied. She could walk like that to any far distance without minding whether she had dresses on her skin or not. She had never put on any shoes, neither had she any idea how it was. In her days, they were counting manillas and she knew nothing about the type of money we are now using. All these are some of the things that differentiate my life from hers.

Life has improved in many ways more than the days when I was young. People are educated and nearly everybody can tell the value of education now. When I was young people walked in bush tracks and nobody knew anything about motors and bicycles. If anybody wanted to travel a long distance, it always lasted such a person many weeks before he got to the place because all the distance would be done by foot. That was the reason why many people never liked travelling out to distant places. During that time, people were often killed like goats if they went contrary to any law of the village. Slave dealing was still common because they thought that could be the easiest way of training disobedient children. These days such things had been abolished due to the wide experience that people get consequential to adequate qualifications.

Commentary

Although this woman is an Ikwere Ibo, her treatment as 'home daughter' is not different from what she might expect among the Ibibio. If an Ijaw, she would be less likely to be cheated of her birthright of farmland.

It would appear paradoxical to call this person a 'home daughter' since she has spent less time at 'home' than any other woman in this collection. However, it is often the case that such a daughter is dedicated to the care of her father in all domestic duties, besides the provision of heirs.

She is healthy, and well-dressed in modern fashion. Though no longer young, and officially a bartender, she and another woman of her age rent a house between them where they are well known to be carrying on the business of their youth.

The magic water-pot

I was born in Okoho in Eket Province. I was born about sixty-two years ago in the family of a certain chief in Eket Province.

I was a girl of about ten years of age when I stayed with my senior sister who was married to a certain trader at Ifiayong in Uruan district. My sister whom I stayed with was married for five years before she became a mother. When she was under pregnancy for two months she went into the fattening room as it was then the custom. It was a surprise to see that after my sister had stayed there for six months she became seriously ill and not very long after she died in the fattening room. After one year from the time my sister died, my parents were in great sympathy with my sister's husband for having missed his wife immediately after a heavy bride-price had been paid on her behalf. My parents called my sister's husband and asked him to choose another girl in the family in place of his late wife. The man refused the idea of choosing any of the wife's sisters in marriage because, though that was our custom, it was not so in his custom. My parents having known his rank as a trader in those days, begged him to accept me in marriage and he later accepted. This took place while I was between twelve and eleven years of age. Not very long, I was pregnated and things started to be clear to me as a housewife. I was then made to understand that it was my husband who killed my sister in what is known as 'Free Medicine'. A certain pot was shown to me to fill with water every morning and this was the type of job my sister did in the house. I later discovered that any day that I forgot to fill water in that pot, I must have a serious fever except I remembered to fill in the pot before I became normal. The pot was also kept in his room and no other person was allowed to get into the room other than the two of us. As I never understood the value of that pot, I told those who were older than myself, and they told me the harm that the pot would do to me if I did not divorce my husband immediately. I started seeing many changes in my life as other people said and I decided to divorce him to safeguard my life. I was also made to understand that in the case of five of his wives who died, this money producing juju was the cause of their death and that was the reason why people refused him wives in his own village except he went out to places where people knew very little about him. I divorced him immediately I was put to bed for my first son.

My present husband is my second husband. When I decided to divorce my husband, I started negotiating with him so that immediately I divorced my husband I stayed only three months with my parents before he came out to marry me.

My husband is still living. Though he has many grown-up children, yet he is not all that old because his late father married his first wife for him while he was only fifteen years of age. He is a fisherman and he did this from his youth till a few years ago when he stopped. He has got two canoes of his own and hired some people to control them for him.

I have three co-wives and I am the fourth. Three of them are younger than myself and I am the oldest of them.

As a senior wife, I am always given a due respect. We do everything in common and each of us is kind to one another. Any of us can open her mate's door and take anything she likes without minding whether the owner of the house is there or not. If the owner of the house comes back to be informed of such, she could not be annoyed because she takes her mate as herself. Of course where more than one woman marries one man, there is always jealousy between them. In this case there is jealousy but not much because if our husband wants to give us dresses he must buy the same colour for four of us. As a senior wife, I always advise my husband to share anything among his wives in order of seniority. As for dresses, I arrange with my husband to suit every wife so that none of us might complain that her own is inferior to another.

When I was a small girl, I lived with my parents until later I went and stayed with my late sister at her husband's house. I went back to my parents after my sister had died. The next place I stayed was my former husband's house and lastly where I am living at present.

Where I am living is where I like best. If I did not like here, it means I could not have chosen staying here even from the time I was not as old as this. I so much like staying here because I have got children and nothing can distract my interest from the compound again.

Yes, even though my present husband is not my first husband since I was born, yet I can describe my life as a happy one. The reason is that I have children for my husband and at present I cannot be maltreated by my husband as long as my children are living.

I have not got a fixed handwork. When I was a girl I was selling crawfish for my mother. When I married, I was doing some farming and petty trading. When my children became grown-ups they told me not to worry myself so much in doing some petty trade. They have been giving me some money for my food to enable me earn a living.

I have three male children and six females. They were thirteen children in number but four died. All of them are coupled with fifteen children, but four died. Some of my daughters married into wicked families. This caused the loss of many children of theirs.

The happiest time in my life was when I was staying with my sister in her husband's house. During that time, I never knew that to marry a husband was not a simple thing. I lived a care-free life and all I knew was to eat my food at any time I desired. Whether there was food in the house or not, it never disturbed me because I knew that as far as my sister was in, she must see that everybody ate satisfactorily. It was when I married that I knew that to be a housewife in Ibibio land was not a mere words of mouth but a life full of responsibilities. We had not been having food money from our husband rather we fed our husbands with our money with the little we had from the farm.

I should say, when I divorced my husband, it was an unhappy time for me because we had no quarrel of any kind. I thought that I would not marry again in life. Even though I was trying to safeguard my life, yet I was feeling very sad within myself.

The most interesting thing I can well remember was the time my second daughter wedded with her husband. Even though I was not the person wedded, yet I was very happy because my own daughter had achieved a better position in life than I did. There is one saying that reads, 'when it is good with a female tortoise, it is also good with a male one'. As I was married into a polygamous family I would be very happy to see any of my daughters owning her husband alone. There were many disadvantages to a woman whose husband marries more than one wife. It means that some of the difficulties that many co-wives could give to one another my daughter would not encounter them because the husband marries her alone.

I say with experience that it is a bad thing for a woman when the husband has more than one wife, because she could not have any control over the husband especially if she is the junior wife. Anything presented to the junior wives must first of all be discussed with the senior wife. The wife cannot express her feelings to the husband as she should because she would feel that no plan would be carried out without the consent of the senior wife. The wife would not have freedom over anything in the house because she knows if she does so, others might start creating some misunderstanding or jealousy. Her children would not be properly cared for, and they would not be given adequate education to help them earn a better living. It does not mean that the husband wouldn't like to do something better for his own children but he cannot make two ends meet due to many difficulties he has. The wife would not gain much love and interest from the husband because the husband shares his love among other wives.

My grandmother was kindest to me, but since she died nobody else again. It is the custom that, when the girl is married out of the parent's family, their parent's family does not show much of their kindness to her any longer because they know any good thing done to her would be enjoyed by the family of the husband.

I have no good friends outside my family since all my age groups died. The modern women are not reliable and none of them would like to associate with me since I am not their age group.

I allowed my sons and daughters to choose partners for themselves instead of choosing for them as my parents did. Though my mother was older than myself, yet I have known many better things than she did during her time. If anybody offend me I can pardon the person and at the same time forget about it, but in my mother's case that has never been the case. I can dress in a neater way than my mother did. In my mother's days little was known about the value of money but now I can make good use of the money I have than my mother did. I at times lent some fishermen my money so that at the end of every year, if the money I gave to one fisherman was one pound, I will expect my interest to be ten shillings plus the actual money I gave making one pound ten shillings.

Life has got a better stand than the days I was young. In those days, people were under the primitive society and the standard of living was very slow and backward. People walked in bush tracks which were along thick forest and there was nothing like the type of main roads we have now. People were not living in a community as we are now living. Some spaces that can occupy ten houses these days were in those days occupied with only two or three houses. Lands were often wasted for other minor purposes instead of building houses for people to live together. Twin mothers were regarded as the most sinful women and their lives were always in danger. The worship of juju was very common and it was regarded as the best thing that can earn anybody a better living. Bride-prices were very low and this awarded freedom of having as many wives as possible. Now everything has been improved for a better standard of living.

Commentary

The nature of the divorce of this wife from her first husband is significant inasmuch as it was permitted after the birth of her first son, implying that she had satisfied the conditions of the bride-price paid when her deceased sister became pregnant. Among many differing ethnies, bride-price could be more appropriately described as heir-price.

Although senior wife to a husband who is still alive, she lives (together with her goats) in a small house in her son's compound, and although her children provide her with European dress, she prefers to go naked at home, and wear a simple cloth tied at the shoulder when she goes out.

A reprieved man's daughter

I was born at Nung Ukot Ikono, a village under Uyo Province.

I cannot exactly tell my age but, according to my parents, I was said to have been born in the year when a certain woman got missing in an attempt to cross the track leading to their compound while 'Ekpo' society were performing their dances. It was the law then that, if a woman was seen while the dances were performed, such woman's head must be cut off and kept before the Ekpo shrine as a remembrance of disobedience. That place was also a secret place to women because it was where all secrets concerning 'Ekpo' were always performed.

It was then our custom that when a girl was very young, she must be given to marriage before she was up to the age of puberty. It was believed that, if the girl was left in the mother's house till she was fully matured, other men might covet her and through regular contact she might be got with child and put her mother to shame. In those days, when a girl conceived in the parents' house while she was not yet married she would be put into a song and disgraced. Both the girl and the parents would be considered the most unmannered people. These were the reasons I was given to marriage while I was very young. I can still remember that when I was given to marriage, I did not develop any breast.

However, my first husband died while I was almost ten years old in his house. By then, I did not even get my first child. After his death, I stayed outside his house for three years but after that, a daughter of my present husband came and married me to her father as her mother was then too old to give birth to children. My husband is still living, though he is older than myself.

When I married him newly he was a palm wine tapper, and he did some palm fruit cutting and petty native farming. Now that all veins in him are getting too weak, he can no longer do any kind of serious work.

I am the only wife of the man since his first and second wives died. When these women died I encouraged him to marry another woman who could be assisting me in the farm work. He ignored the idea of a second wife because he thought he was too old to approach anybody for marriage.

Where I am living at the moment is where I like best. I am not bound for any place again for I am already old. Even if I happen to go back to my father's compound today, nobody would accept me back, because there would be no room for me.

I can describe my life as a happy one because I have able children who will bury me when I die. There is nothing as happy as that because children are the glory of any married woman. If a woman stays without any child in the husband's house, there would be no peace of any kind with the wife and such a life would be described as an unhappy life. Even though such a woman could be outwardly happy, yet inwardly she would be very unhappy when she would consider some of her mates whom perhaps they were fattening the same year. In my own case, it is not so because my children are my pride. This has been the main reason why I consider my life to be a happy one.

I have been doing some petty trading and farming for most of my life. I started trading at the time when all things were very cheap and with very little profit. In those days, I often bought a big bag of crawfish now worth Ten Pounds for only a Pound Ten and with a little profit of about two shillings for a whole bag. I could still remember that in those days, when I often brought the crawfish back, I had always shared it to my relatives and neighbours because very little was known about the good uses of money.

I have now a male child and three daughters with ten grandsons and daughters. Many of my grandchildren have also got many children.

The happiest time I can well remember in my life was the time my late father succeeded in a murder case preferred against him by the inhabitants of Ukpom, a village under Abak Division. The person who was murdered was the late chief of Ukpom in connection with the land dispute that the people of a certain village had with those at Ukpo under Abak. My father was alleged to have accepted some money and to have been commissioned to kill the people concerned.

Judgment was almost passed on him before it was revealed that it was one of the man's brothers who killed him in revenge for killing the brother's wife by means of witchcraft. When my father was freed from the case, some native rites and plays were performed to welcome him back a clean and truthful person. I consider that moment to be the happiest time because after all the heavy punishments we the entire family received, God revealed the truth and my father was set free.

The unhappiest time in my life was when my junior sister died while in the fattening room. The death occurred as a result of influenza that attacked her while in the fattening room.

The most interesting thing that happened to me was the time I exposed my daughter out of the fattening room. The husband arranged everything to suit me according to the custom. It was then the custom that when the first daughter of somebody is given to marriage, certain rites must be observed in honour of the mother-in-law. Thus he did a sort of honour to my person and I can speak boldly in this type of gathering without any shame. It was always the belief that, if the mother-in-law was not given her own share when the daughter was married, it means the mother-in-law had not possessed sufficient money to feed the son-in-law according to the custom the first day that the bride-price was paid to the father.

In my opinion, I say it is a good thing for a woman when the husband has more than one wife because other wives would help to multiply the family more than one wife could do. Many wives help in feeding the husband more than one wife could do. In such cases women are often responsible for the feeding of the husband. Whether a woman was rich or not, it does not concern the husband so long as he eats regularly. If the husband gets annoyed with any of the co-wives, other co-wives call help to bring back peace among them instead of exposing them.

At the moment, the only person in my family who is good to me is my uncle. He proves a good father, both in need and in deeds, since my father died. People in my husband's family always treat me fairly because of him. If I am badly treated in the marriage home, he would come and make them feel that as long as he lives I cannot be badly treated. During the time of harvesting, he usually gives me my own share of the yams as he does to his own wives. Even if I have financial difficulties, he is the only person I will first approach. Beside him, I could have been left stranded since my father died.

I have friends but I don't put my trust on all of them. Many of them are those in the same society with me, and that is why they are interested in me. All of them are old women as I am and they cannot render any help to me. Of course, they usually visit me at their convenience as I can also do with them. We are fond of telling funny stories to one another, and that is all we could do.

My life differs from that of my mother in many ways. Most of the things I see in this present world were not existing in my mother's days. In their days all things were done in primitive ways. People knew very little about the value of money because they knew no other way of making good use of money other than buying of their goods, marrying wives for their sons and storing some in their houses so that it could be stored on their graves for them when they died. During my mother's days, children were not educated and little was known of the benefits of education and almost every member of the society regarded it as a white man's institution meant to serve as a weapon for the suppression of the Africans. I can still remember that when Qua Iboe Mission opened a school newly in my village, about twenty years ago, teachers went from house to house to drag children to school. Even though there was no fees to be paid, but still many parents hid their children, because they thought if they allowed their children to go to school, from there heavy tax would be levied according to the number of children.

The type of thing that my mother used as basin for going to farm and market were made of cane with some wood at the bottom to help them carry on the head. Now that all things are changed, enamel basins are used both for young and old women, both for farm work and also for market.

Many kinds of food that I have been seeing my daughter-in-law cook for her husband were not known in those days. I have also eaten more delicious food than my mother did because my own children helped to improve my life to suit the condition of life now.

Indeed, life has got better these times than the time I was young. Most of the things have changed since people started knowing the value of education. Even though I was born into a society of semi-primitive people whose hearts were governed by fear and superstition, yet I can say boldly that, white people have now made people to understand things clear and easier for people through education.

Commentary

An attempt was made to ascertain this woman's age by investigating the death of the victim of the Ekpo. Significantly, the elderly men reported that so many women died at the hands of this society in those days that they could not say which case she referred to. The opinion of her neighbours was that she was about sixty at the time of the interview.

Another significant detail of this story is that her marriage to her second husband was arranged by his daughter. She in her turn recruited a further wife at a time when her husband himself was unwilling on account of age. It would appear that polygamy is more suited to the household of an elderly patriarch who is less likely to stir up jealousy among his wives.

A chief's widow

I was born at Afia Ngil but married at Western Itam. After my first husband died, I was married again by one of the oldest chiefs of Ifa who was the senior man in charge of a certain society known as 'Ekong'. In those days, 'Ekong' was often played like 'Ekpe' society but a small shrine was often built in front of the chief's compound in charge of 'Ekong' so that any stranger coming into the village will know at once that the owner of that compound was the only chief in that village in charge of 'Ekong' society.

I married my first husband immediately I was out from the fattening room. In those days it was the custom in my village that a girl must not be given to marriage except she had been fattened. Any parents who gave their daughter to marriage before she was fattened were always asked to pay some fine of seven cases of drink and seven she-goats, and all other ingredients to cook the goats. This law was so strong that nobody no matter how poor he was had ever given his daughter for marriage when she was not yet fattened. And this always took place when a girl was between fifteen and seventeen years of age.

I married my first husband who died many years ago before I came to marry my last husband who also died. When my first husband died I stayed for five years before I married my second husband. My last husband has also been dead about six years.

My first husband was a native doctor but my last husband was doing some petty farming but he was a chief in charge of 'Ekong' society. He was so much benefited in taking charge of the society because through that, he was able to have both drink, chickens and many other eatable things free of charge when ever the members came for their weekly worship or sacrifice before the shrine.

My last husband had three wives and I was his last wife.

I respected the other wives because they were my seniors. Even though my husband was so much interested in me than other wives, yet I did not reveal the love through my actions to my co-wives because they would have found one way or the other to do me harm. They were kind to me and my children whom I delivered for my first husband. Those children were small when my first husband died and that was the reason why I came along with them to my second marriage home. As time went on they (my co-wives) noticed that my husband loved me more than the two of them, therefore the two of them started to be jealous of me. And before that time, I also used some preventions in case they planned ill of me.

As my father was a fisherman, I had been going to the fishing port with him in those days. Since I started to marry, I have not stayed in any other place than my husband's houses.

When I never married, I liked to stay at the fishing port more than I liked staying with my mother at home. At the fishing port I had plenty fish to cook any type of food, whereas in the house my mother could only buy some small quantity of crawfish for her food. Secondly, my mother was very economical and she never wanted to use her manillas for fish except my father comes back to give plenty fish free of charge to her.

During that time, my life was a happy one, because as the only female child of my father, he always give me the lion share in anything I needed from him. I never enjoyed my life as a happy one in my first husband's house because the man was too poor. When I married my second husband newly I was extremely happy in life because I had many things I needed free of charge. I ate chickens and goat meats as I liked and I was very healthy.

I had farming as my occupation when I started life as a housewife till this time.

I had three children for my first husband but I have not got any child for my last husband.

The happiest time of my life was during the year my senior sister came and refund the bride-price my former husband paid on my behalf to his brother who wanted to kill me because I refused him for marriage after his brother's death. As my senior sister was a wealthy trader, she refunded the money that was paid on my behalf to my brother-in-law and that was the day I left the compound to go and stay with my parents. My parents were the people who collected my bride-price but they had no money to pay back to my brother-in-law and that was the reason why my senior sister took up the risk herself so that my life be secured.

My unhappiest time was when my senior sister died after a three days' sickness. She was my right-hand person and since she died, life became a bitter one with me.

The most important thing that happened to me was when my second husband died. Before my second husband died he called the three of us, and his belongings were shared to all of us according to his wish. If my husband had not done so, I should have been too much cheated after his death especially as I did not have any child for him.

I do not myself object to polygamy; it does not mean that when a man has more than one wife, any of his wives should have cause to complain. In my opinion, I say it is not a bad thing for a woman when her husband has more than one wife. Whether one's husband has twenty or more wives, that does not prevent him to love one or two out of them provided they are better mannered than the rest.

I have many friends outside my family in whom I can confide. All of them are from my village and are married in this village as well as myself.

Most of the people from my father's family who were kindest to me have all died. I have not got anybody again in the family who is kind to me.

My life is much the same as that of my mother because I am not educated as my mother was, but there are many good changes in life this time than when I was young. Many people have now become Christians these days because people are no longer dwelling under primitive control. Education has brought in many new changes from the days when I was young.

Commentary

Though this woman has been twice a widow, she is nevertheless notorious in her village for wearing widow's weeds for a much longer period than is now customary, rejecting all dresses given her by her daughter-in-law. She has never been converted to Christianity, and keeps a shrine in her room for the protection of her family.

She has very few possessions, and, judging by her appearance and her nostalgia for her fish-eating days, insufficient to eat.

The money-doubler's widow

I was born at Ekim in Uruan Division under a polygamous family of one of the late chiefs of Ekim.

In our days we were under the primitive rule and everything was backward and very primitive. Nobody had any idea that it could have been of any good use if children's births were registered. Rather, wine palms or plantains were often planted to mark the date of the child's circumcision which always occurred seven days after the child's birth. People in those days often counted their years according to the number of years that such palms or plantains were planted and when it stayed too long, they forgot the actual time and consequently lost remembrance of the birth day. People also usually counted the year of farming and their age according to the number of years that a particular land was fallowed before it was again cultivated. In my own case, nobody took notice of all these things because my father had so many wives with countless children, and three or four wives could deliver in one day, so it was impossible for him to take note as others did by then.

I was very young when I was given in marriage and I could still remember that when I was married my husband had been buying only a yard of cloth for my dresses. In other words, I was between eight and nine years of age before I was taken in marriage. In those days, girls were often given in marriage while they were so young so that they might be trained by their husbands before they were up to the age of marriage. It was believed that if a girl was not trained by the husband, she might not be able to know what the husband hated and that which he liked.

I have been married only once since I was born.

My husband is not still alive. He died many years ago. He left twelve women to mourn him and many of them went back to their fathers' compounds while others married other men in the same family leaving only three of us who stayed in my husband's compound because we were advanced.

He was a native doctor and later became an occultist when he realized there was not much money in his former business. He was fond of performing wonders, a very good man at money doubling. He could also invoke a dead man to come out of the grave, and deal with him or ask him to prescribe anything that would help him in his job for him.

Most of my co-wives had no children left after my husband's death. At the moment, only three of us are staying in the compound without having married because we were advanced in age when our husband died. Three of us are staying under the control of our children.

As a senior person to them all I am always respected and most of my co-wives were in the same age group with some of my children. As regards kindness, this is always common among women especially where so many women are married by one man who controls them. Nevertheless, jealousy is always the order of the day where many women are married by one man.

Since I grew up I have not been living in any other place than my father's compound and the next place is my husband's compound where I am now staying.

I like to live in my husband's compound with my children. The compound, though my husband was a native doctor, yet, it was well organized and people were taught to live in peace and co-operation. People were not wicked towards one another. In some compounds, you can see that people die like fowls because of the way the owner of the compound plans his well-being at the expense of the compound. My husband was not wicked to other people's children. That was why our compound was always in peace and children grew up to enjoy it till the present time. I like living in my husband's compound. even after my husband's death because I knew that as my husband was not a wicked man, nobody could be wicked to me and even my children. If my husband were to be a wicked and destructive man, I should have gone back to my father's compound after his death. This is one of the reasons why I like the compound up to this present time.

Yes, I describe my life as a happy one because I have children for my late husband. There is nothing that makes a woman happy in the married home like children. Even though my children are not many, but the few I have are the cause of my happiness in my late husband's house and in their family as a whole. Even though my parents were dwelling under the primitive rule and they had no idea of educating me, yet my children have enlightened me and make my life to be the most happy life among those of my sisters. My husband came to realize, through a brother who was then a spiritual Church preacher, the glories that one could rightly enjoy in the education of one's children and for this reason my first son and daughter were sent to school, and through these two people my life had many changes from that of some women.

I have been a farmer since I grew up in my husband's house. I have also been doing some petty trading. When my husband was alive I had been assisting him in collecting some herbs for him and this occupied most of my time. It was through this method that I was able to know some of the treatment for children's sickness, such as convulsion, measles and other minor treatments.

I have three male children and two females. Two of them are fishermen while the other man is a government worker. My children are all married with children and grandchildren.

My happiness in life started when all my children grew up to be responsible men and women. It was a rule in the family that when children were up to the age of going to school, the first son of every wife was always trained, so that he might be the person to look after his mother's house. That means, he will be the one responsible for the training of other brothers and sisters. My first son did very well in the school and he came out successfully to help as well. Sons not able to do so well in school left stranded other brothers and sisters because my husband had many responsibilities at hand. Those wives were always very sad and whenever they saw how other children grew up to shoulder the responsibilities of both their mothers, brothers, and sisters, they became very unhappy and disturbed in mind.

The unhappiest time in my life was when my husband died. Though he was old, yet I felt his death because as a father to all, he was the glory of the compound. Since his death, everything has been dislocated and scattered and nobody can control the compound as he did. Though he has responsible sons yet they cannot do half of what the father had been doing.

The most important thing that happened to me was the time I was put into fattening room. Here I was made to eat and grow very fat. I was hidden in the house for two years without seeing my father and my proposed husband. It was the custom that before a girl was out from the fattening room, both the father and the proposed husband must pay a fat sum of money before they came to see her. On the last day, many native plays were staged and even the compound was crowded, I was asked to come and dance. Before I came out, I was well dressed with costly beads and with costly apparels. A handsome and strong young man was also dressed to carry me on his shoulders so that I might not be equal to those walking on the ground. It was an interesting thing as the man came out carrying me on his shoulders with my two legs across his neck, and he started dancing to the beating of the different drums. After dancing in the compound, the man still carried me to the market square and danced the play round the market before going back to my father's compound. This was the day that I first counted my manillas up to an astonishing number of bunches. After all the functions had finished, I was again taken to my husband's house and before this time I was fully mature to be a woman. That was indeed a happy and the most interesting time in my life.

Personally, I believe it is a bad thing for a woman when the husband has more than one wife because she will be the only one caring for her children because the husband has many responsibilities around him. The husband will only be responsible for the supplying of lands for farming, caring for himself and perhaps doing the little he could for the children of other beloved wives. If any of the wives is unfortunate and the husband counted her as a disobedient wife, the husband will not do any good thing to the children of such wives so that the mothers of the children may not be benefited in future. The wife will not have many pieces of land to farm on because all the pieces of land will be shared among the number of wives that the man has and the wives would not have sufficient food as we all depend wholly and entirely on our farms. The wives will not always remain in peace with the husband because other women will find means to blackmail any of the wives they feel that their husband liked most. If any of the wives was wicked, she would find a way to kill anybody in the compound whom she felt the husband loved more than herself. Most unexpected deaths were always caused by some wicked co-wives. These are some of the reasons why I say it is a bad thing for a woman when the husband has more than one wife.

My junior brother has been kindest to me. In any trouble in my marriage home, I usually approach him before any other person. He had been very kind to me without minding that I had been married out of my father's compound. It was the custom that, when a girl was married out of the family, she was always regarded as a stranger whenever she went into the father's compound. In my own case it was not so because my junior brother was highly interested in me.

At the moment, I have no good friend outside my family. All my mates, who were my friends have all died and my sons and daughters are now my friends. There's nothing a friend could do to me which my children could not do to me. Even though those friends of mine who died were so good to me, yet I cannot compare the help that my children give me to their own. My children have helped me in everything possible, especially this time that I cannot do anything so actively again.

Well! There is nothing I can do for my family other than taking care of their children when their mothers are away. As an old woman, my daughters always send their children to me as they know I have not been going out again. In short, I am a nurse to my daughters and I always visit them in turns.

My children have made my life to get changed in many ways. My mother did everything in fear and was controlled by primitive people who knew nothing about education. My mother did everything backwardly because by then there was nobody who could coach her as I have been today. Even though I was not educated, yet my children have also helped to improve my life as the modern world needs. My children have made me to eat many types of food which in days gone by nobody had any idea of such. They have made me to be a church member which in those days my mother knew nothing about any church nor did she belong to any of the Christian societies.

Life in these days is far better than the days I was young. In olden days, parents were responsible for the choosing of husbands for their daughters. They considered those men with many pieces of farm lands to be the best men their daughters could marry so that they might eat satisfactorily, because they thought their daughters cannot have what to eat in a poor family where there were no farm lands. Disobedient children were often sold into slavery and without any government law binding them. People went half naked and regarded dressing as nothing. But in this modern world both men and women consider dressing as one of those things that matters in life. In those days, men had only one method of bobbing their hair, and anybody who bobbed contrary to that was often considered as a disobedient man who considered himself higher than the chiefs of the village, and this type of man was often punished by demanding unwarranted taxes from him. In this modern world men have many types of bobbing their hair and there is nobody to check them.

In those days village chiefs were considered to be the most perfect people. If cases were taken to these chiefs, they wouldn't judge it correctly, rather they judged the case to be in favour of somebody who had influential men behind them so that the chiefs might later have some presents like tobacco and drink from the relatives of the person who succeeded in the case. A poor man was often cheated and was said to be the most disobedient man in the village. In this modern world things like that are not existing, rather they judge cases according to the government law and order.

Commentary

It is interesting to note that this woman underwent circumcision in infancy, either because she belonged to an aristocratic family, or came of Efik stock. It is also clear to see from this story that fattening took place when she had already removed to her husband's house, though her father was still concerned with the expenses.

A village schoolmistress

I am a free-born woman of Anua, a village about two miles to Uyo. I was the daughter of one of the oldest chiefs in 'Edat' family and I was born in 1914 in Use Offat, a small village near my own village. My mother was a native of Use and when she knew that her time was completed, she went and stayed with my grandmother so that she might be encouraged when labour started as that was her first time she was going to experience such pains.

I did not marry early as I was staying with one of my father's sons who served the early Catholic missionaries who were then organizing St Luke's Hospital, Anua. Through the help of my brother, our father was made to know the benefit that one could derive from the training of both men and women. People thought it was a mere waste of money to train women but yet my father's first son was prepared to face many difficulties so see that any child born into that particular family was sent to school. When I was ten years of age I was sent to school until I passed my form one as it was then called. My father, who thought he could not further my education any more, sent me to his son who was serving the missionaries and the son recommended me to the people who employed me as a maid for only fifteen shillings a month. I served them for one year and I later gained admission into the Hope Waddel Training Institute, Calabar. I completed my course in 1932 when I joined as one of the teachers in the school. It was then that I came across my late husband and we started as friends.

He was then an agent to one of the companies in Calabar and he had been visiting the school compound to advertise his business. Even though he was not from the same village with me, I liked him for his social life. In 1937, I took him to introduce to my parents and not very long afterwards we wedded in the Catholic Church, Anua. This marriage was indeed a coincidence: as I was negotiating with my proposed husband at Calabar, one of his brothers was also negotiating to marry one of my sisters at home. Nobody knew of this until on the day my husband came to pay the bride-price his brother who negotiated to marry my sister came with him and it was too late for either myself or my sister to refuse these two brothers in marriage.

My late husband was my only husband since I was born. And since he died in 1964, I have never negotiated to marry any man. He died on December 25th, 1964. He was a produce buyer and also on the Board of Directors of the Ibibio State Union in Calabar, and he was also one of the Branch Directors of the Rosicrucian Order in Calabar township as a whole.

Though my husband married so many wives, yet he divorced them before we wedded. One of his wives is one of the richest women in the whole of Calabar township. She was the one who gave birth to my husband's first son who was formerly the Assistant Head Postmaster at Kano.

Even though they were not under the control of my husband when I married the man, yet as an intelligent woman, they were respectful to me when they visited their children's father. It is their custom that if Calabar women are divorced, they must still keep visiting the man at any time they liked provided they had children for such husbands. The Calabar ways of doing things are very different from what we Ibibios do. They used to be very kind to me each time they visited my husband who was sometime their husband as well. They did all these kindnesses so that whenever they were away I might speak good of them to the husband so that during their next visit, the husband might give them much money for the feeding of his children. They had never showed me any jealousy since they had been coming to me.

During my life I have stayed at Anua and later at Calabar. I like living at Calabar because my husband has a plot* here. Secondly, I was brought up in Calabar and I prefer staying here to any other place.

Even though my husband died about three years ago, and all my relatives died leaving very few, yet I still describe my life as a happy one as God has given me children. Secondly, I am still teaching in the Edgerley Secondary Girls' School, Calabar. Though I have many responsibilities as a widow, yet with the help of my children I can still manage my life.

* A building site.

I have been a teacher since I left the College. Teaching work is also a nice job for women.

I have three daughters and two sons. My first daughter is a tutor at Ifuho Girls' Secondary School, Ikot Ekpene. My junior daughter is a staff nurse at the General Hospital, Calabar. The third one was learning typing and shorthand and most unfortunately for her she was pregnated by a certain man who is now maintaining her. My first son has not yet got anything doing since he passed his First School-leaving Certificate examination. My second son chose to be a Reverend father and this is his first year at the seminary. I have no grandchildren yet.

The happiest time I can remember was the time I wedded with my late husband. It was indeed one of the best organized weddings in the history of Anua. Much money was spent and we did it to the satisfaction of any born Catholic who had an idea of how wedding could be done. I can say that such a costly wedding has been very scarce in the history of my village.

The unhappiest time was when my husband died on December 25th, 1964. The death was indeed a terrible one. He was with us on that December morning trying to arrange things for the children when he collapsed and died at the spot. Since he died everything in life seemed to be against me and since then I have been very sick. To prove that my late husband was all and all for me, and since he died everything dislocated in the house, I gave an order to my children that the main door leading to his main parlour must always be closed. Since they carried his corpse through that door to his home town for burial, nobody has ever made attempt of opening the door. Rather, we choose passing through the backyard into the house. This door really proved that since the owner of the house died, till this present time, his death has kept the whole family in darkness.

The most interesting thing that happened to me, was the time I was appointed the head of the Ibibio Women's Wing at Calabar. I was very happy because I was a junior woman to some of those who were not selected. Of course it was through my husband that they gave me this post.

In my opinion, I say it is not a good thing for a woman when her husband has more than one wife. The first wife would not gain full respect and prestige from the husband due to the confusion other women would cause. The husband would have many more responsibilities than he should have during the time he married many wives.

Once I had so many members of my family who were good to me but all have died leaving me alone. Also, I have had many good friends outside my family in whom I can confide. Many of them are expatriates from the Catholic mission to which I belong.

Most of them help me by giving me useful advice. There is a certain woman doctor whom I knew during her stay at Anua with the husband who awarded my junior daughter a scholarship to a secondary school. Most of these ladies like me due to my good manners and behaviour. I also have been helping them by doing some kind work to them as well.

I think I am more fortunate than my mother: I am trained and my mother was not. My mother believed in superstition and she knew nothing about Christianity, nor did she want anybody to tell her anything about it. She thought one could not be safe without being under the protection of any juju. Her way of living was very backward and primitive.

Commentary

This story is interesting in that it illustrates one of the tragic results of the superimposition of Christianity upon local tradition, i.e. the divorce of the 'so many wives' by the Calabar man regardless of their children, when he wished to undergo a Catholic marriage. Fortunately, in this case, the separation does not appear to have been final.

A prosperous wife

I was born at Opobo under the area of King JaJa of Opobo. The reason why one side of Opobo belonged to King JaJa was because King JaJa was bought from Iboe land and sold into slavery to one of the chiefs of Opobo. As time went on, the chief made JaJa to be the king of one side of Opobo town, and this happened as a price of his good services to the chief. That was how King JaJa came from Iboe land to rule a certain area in Opobo land while the other side belonged to the Ibibios.

As for my age, that is what I cannot make out as my parents were pure illiterates and nothing was known about the value of keeping children's birth records.

I started life in the house of my first husband immediately I was out of the fattening room. This took place when I was using only two yards of cloth. We married for nine years and the marriage ended in divorce as I had no children for him. Because of this, other co-wives of mine became very contemptuous of me and there was no peace between me and my husband.

I married my present husband after that husband had divorced me for six months. But to my greatest surprise, I was pregnated between a space of two months in my new husband's house.

My last husband is still alive. He is a contractor at the Methodist hospital, Ituk Mbang under Uyo Province. He joined the work since 1918 as a labourer according to my husband. Through his good work the hospital authorities promoted him to be the chief contractor in charge of all washings.

We are two wives, but I am his second wife. As a junior person I always give my co-wife full respect. I am always kind to her and her children despite the fact that we do not live in the same house. There is no jealousy among us because two of us have got able children to care for us.

As I had already said, my home town is Opobo, but my late father brought my late brother and myself while he was establishing a trade here with his friend. When my father brought me to this town I was a small girl and I never experienced life outside my father's house until I married my first husband. When my former husband divorced me, I went back to my father's house until my present husband came out and married me.

I prefer where I am at the moment to my former husband's house. The people of this place are very good with strangers and they have sufficient lands for the planting of cassava which is our staple food. When my father died, the people of this village provided a piece of land to bury my father without minding that he was not a native. My father's second and third wives, who were also brought to this village by my late father, were buried here and all the lands were given free of charge by the natives.

My life is indeed a happy one in my present husband's house because I have got children for him which I was suffering for the lack of in the house of my first husband whom I married. My children have earned a better living and through their help my life is greatly improved. My husband also has sufficient money to maintain his family and all his daughters are married by responsible men. Some of the unmarried daughters are also doing better jobs.

I have been a trader for most of my years and I trade on crawfish only.

I have seven male children and two females, with fifteen grand-children.

There were two happy occasions in my life. One was during the time I came out of the fattening room, and the other was when two of us, myself and my husband, were freed from a murder case which was preferred against us. It was the custom that, if a girl is put into the fattening room, she must eat as much as she can, whether she likes it or not, so that on the exposing day she might appear very fat and slick. By being so, the parents of the girl will be very happy and many presents will be given to them by well wishers. The parents of the girl will receive many words of honour as regards their services to their daughter. As for fatness, I broke a record for that and till this present time nobody has been as fat as I was. As regards a murder case which we had, we wasted all that we had and lastly we came out free.

My unhappiest time in life was during the time I married my former husband for many years without any child.

The most interesting thing that happened to me was during the time I had my first child for my present husband. When I remembered how I suffered in my former husband's house because of having no child for him, I became very happy within myself and I consider that period to be the most interesting moments in my life. It was indeed an interesting period because all those who talked ill of me in connection with my barrenness had changed and used the same mouth to praise God in the wonderful thing they saw in me, that was 'pregnancy' after people had lost their hope.

It is a good thing for a women when the husband has more than one wife. The wife will not have regular visits to other men's wives which perhaps might not create an impression to the husband of such women. When a woman has many co-wives, her own children will have many brothers and sisters of the same father to play with, instead of going outside to create some troubles with other people's children. By having many co-wives, one will learn to be social with her co-wives and children will grow up to copy how their mothers lived in peace, co-operation and sociality with her co-wives.

My last sister has been most considerate to me. It does not mean that she has been giving me many things, but she takes me as her real mother. She visits me as she should do to either my mother or my father who died. She does not have any discrimination on my own children, rather she takes them as her own children as well. I value more her good manners than a fat sum of money she could give to me.

Now I am above the age of having friends outside my family rather I have my children as my friends. My children are the people helping me both in finance and otherwise. They care very well about my good health. I do not help them in any way because I was the one maintaining them till they grew up to be responsible people. They are now expected to help me in any way possible as I am getting weak and older.

My life has been a different one from that of my mother because I have got trained children who educate me on how to live to suit with the present way of life. I enjoy more delicious food than my mother did. I dress in a better and neatful way than she did and enjoy many more improvements in life than my mother did.

Indeed, life has got better these days than the days I was young because of highly qualified men and women who helped to bring in civilization into our village. People are made to understand anything that is worth doing more than it was in days gone by. People have freedom to do anything they feel will be of benefit to them.

Commentary

This lady, who is fat, dark and elegant despite being in her middle sixties, lives in the twenty-roomed house built by her husband for his two wives and their children.

She has amassed enough money to pay bride-price for her eldest son, a carpenter, and has impressed her neighbours by purchasing a bicycle for her daughter-in-law.

She has a full social life and is a member of the Methodist Church.

A bitter woman

I was born at Ibesilymo, one of the small villages in Uyo Province.

I am fifty-seven years old. As I grow up to see my baptism certificate, my father was a local preacher in the Methodist Church of Nigeria. With the little knowledge he had as a preacher, he was able to keep my birth certificate. He was brought up in one of the evening classes which was conducted by one of the Methodist Mission teachers whose duty was to teach people how to sing and read the Bible for the benefit of the Church. They had one book known as 'Ikpat ke Ikpat', meaning step by step. With this little book, they were able to read Bible and perhaps write their names. Though my father was not educated yet he can speak pidgin English very well. If you happen to hear him speak, you will find it difficult to understand some of the words used because it is the type of English that reigned during their days.

The man to whom I am married at the moment was not to be my husband but, due to some unforeseen circumstances, I had to manage him as a husband.

He employed me at the age of seven to his second wife as a nurse-maid to her son. I stayed with them till the wife gave birth to three children with the previous one making four. As time went on, my master started to be interested in me till very unfortunately I became pregnant. Though my parents willingly gave me over to them as a nursemaid yet they did not appreciate the idea. There was no remedy to this, so I had to accept my master in marriage at the age of thirteen. I have not been married more than once.

My husband is still living and he looks younger. He married a new young girl during the last two years and this can prove that he is still praying to stay longer if this could be within his own power.

He is a palm wine tapper and this helps him much. With this he has been able to buy two canoes for people mainly dealing in smuggling goods. This also produces much money to him. If Customs were to give chance, I think by now he could have done something better from that source.

At the moment we are twelve wives as four have left. Some of them are respectful and some are very insulting. Some of the modern girls who have been newly married are always very insulting and I don't regard that as anything because we live separately. Some of my mates are very kind to me, but many of them don't like staying with others. You find jealousy being very rampant among the younger groups. As for the older women, there is no such thing among us because we all are used to any condition. There is much jealousy among the junior ones who are newly married into the family.

Apart from my mother's house, this has been my second place to stay since I was born.

I like staying in my husband's compound because it is where I started life from my youth.

I don't describe my life as a happy one because since I took my husband, I have been suffering. My husband right from the time I married him newly, had never maintained me in the way other men are doing. During the time of farming I had to hire labourers myself to clear the bush for me. I clothe myself, and look for my daily food. I use my own money in feeding my husband instead of demanding from him. You may say that it was the way people were doing in those days but my own has become too much. Since from the time I married him newly he has never bought a new dress for me until the previous one had all torn to rags. It is over ten years now I don't have a new dress from him. Those are the reasons I consider my life an unhappy one.

I have been trading on oil since I married him. In those days I had been buying oil from the local women and then going to sell it at Nwaziba Beach. I usually purchased a tin of oil at the rate of 4*s* 6*d* and go there to sell to the Germans who were trading there, at the rate of 5*s* or 5*s* 3*d* at times. Since the Germans went away, I had been selling at Uyo up to the present time when produce dealers come right into the village to buy oil and fill in big drums.

I had five sons and one daughter but most have died leaving me with only a son and three grandchildren.

The unhappiest time in my life was the time all my children died one after the other after they had all grown up. I don't know what might have caused their death but all I know is that many people in the family practise witchcraft and the only person who was suspected of doing the practice revealed before he died.

Since I grew up to know myself, I have never had a happy time. I started suffering from my youth and it has ended just like that.

No interesting thing has ever happened to me.

In my opinion I say it is not a good thing for a woman when her husband has more than one wife. The wife will not be well cared for because the husband has got many. The wife will not be loved by the husband as he should to a wife. In sickness or in trouble the husband will not render much help because he finds the means that one wife should go so that a new one might be fixed in. The children will be left under the care and control of the mother especially if the husband has not the slightest love for the mother. If care is not taken the mother may be responsible for the children's education to the low standard she can afford. All these, I am referring to myself and to any other person who has the same star with me.

Nobody has been kind to me. Since the death of my children people accused me to be the cause of their death. Since then I decided never to associate with anybody. I have nobody outside my family in whom I lay my trust,

Nobody helps me in any way. I am the only person responsible for all my affairs.

As I haven't got help from anybody, I don't help anyone. I had at first been showing some interest and kindness to a certain woman in my husband's family, but since I discovered that her love was from the lips I put a stop to it.

My life has no great difference from that of my mother because my mother suffered much in the married home as I did. Though there are more changes in life today than in my mother's days yet where life seems to be against me, I don't enjoy the changes in life as some of my mates do.

Life has got better this time than my mother's days because civilization has brought into the world many good changes in life. People value education this time more than any other thing, and this has greatly helped to improve the outlook of the people. Because of education, many magnificent buildings are set up around every corner of the village now. In days gone by, people did not know the value of hospitals, clinics, good markets, good roads and many others. People did not value women's education in days gone by because they thought women cannot control themselves in any school without being got with child. But now people are doing secondary schools, higher schools and universities. Such schools that were mainly for sons of rich men has this days become primary schools for daughters of able and unable men alike. All these things prove that life has got better than when I was young.

The barren wife

I was born at Ifiet Ekim, a bushy village under Uruan clan, Uyo Province. I was first of all married at Etoi clan in Uyo Province.

I am sixty-one years of age. I was born about ten years before Methodist Mission was brought into our village by a certain man. They had celebrated their golden jubilee about ten years ago, meaning that the church has been fifty years old from the day of the celebration.

I married at the age of seven. It was the custom that a girl must be given to a husband, who will have to stay with the girl until she reaches the age to marry. It was believed that a girl cannot behave well in the husband's house except she is given to the proposed husband to train her on what he likes and what he does not like. This is exactly how I was given to marriage by my parents.

My present husband is my second husband since I was born. My first husband divorced me because I had no child for him. We married for twelve years and ended in divorce due to lack of children to him.

My present husband is alive. He was formerly a fisherman but now that he is getting weak he has nothing doing, rather he depends wholly and entirely on his children.

We are five in number, but I am the second wife. Out of the five wives I married him one with my own money as I was not able to give him any child. I married him this lady after I had stayed for seven good years in his house without children. My former husband was the cause of my barrenness because he arranged with a native doctor who prepared some medicine to prevent me from conceiving at an early stage while staying under the training in my husband's house. After preparing the pot of this prevention a matchet was used to open a hole on the wall of the native doctor's house, and inside the hole, the pot was put and it was mudded back to the normal state.

Very unfortunately, after many years, the doctor went to the fishing port, he got ill and died there. His corpse was brought back for burial at home. When time reached that I should start building the family, my husband went to members of the doctor's family to sound their opinions before the wall was open to bring out the prevention pot. The family having agreed, they started searching for the pot, but it was not seen. Three to four years passed, no conception and a search was again conducted, but all efforts made were in vain. At last the whole building had to be damaged on account of this pot, yet it was not seen. A serious quarrel broke out between me and my husband and the quarrel ended in divorce, because the doctor told us that I will not get conceived until the pot was brought out from the wall and broken into pieces before I conceived. Since the thing happened like that, nobody has been able to give me the treatment that could make me conceive. If this news were to be published I think it could so much help young men and women of these days who are fond of preventions.

The lady whom I married to my husband respected me. After about four years, people started misleading her that I was not the mother whom she should respect. As for other co-wives, they have not been respecting me because I have no children as they always say behind me. They are not kind to me because they have known that perhaps I will not be able to pay them back. Jealousy always comes from the farms which I am always given, as they feel the best share is always presented to me.

I first lived in my first husband's house and then in this second one since I was born. I have not stayed in any other place other than these two places. I still like to live in my husband's house because at the moment I cannot roam about again. There is a time for everything.

Life without children is not at all a happy one. Since I grew to womanhood, I have not enjoyed life at all. I ignored everything in life and I am used to any condition in life.

I had been trading on crawfish from my youth till the time I was unable to travel long distance.

The happiest time in my life was the time my mother put me into fattening room. This was the happiest time to me because I was well maintained during the period. On the last day, my mother decorated me with costly beads and also equipped me with house utensils according to the custom.

The unhappiest time in my life was the time I discovered that there was not going to be any remedy for me to get children in life. This was the time that I was praying for death but it went far away from me. I imagined the life of a barren woman and I was disgusted in life. Everything seemed to be against me and I decided taking life as it presented itself to me.

I cannot recall any interesting thing that has happened to me before. All I know is that, since I grew up to womanhood, I have been meeting with many odds and no interesting or important thing has ever happened to me.

In my opinion, it is a good thing for a woman when the husband has more than one wife because the wife will get many co-wives to assist both in farm work and in feeding the husband. The wife will have many co-wives to take care of the compound in case the husband is out for fishing.

My dad had been kindest to me during his life time. Even though other members of the family were against me, but my father had been giving me encouragements in connection with what happened to me. He also spent much of his money to find out whether there could be any remedy for me to get at least one child for my former husband.

At the moment I have two friends outside my family who are very reliable. They are also housewives as I am. One of them had no child at first but after several efforts she was able to become fruitful.

They have been helping me with good pieces of advice. They have been conducting me to many native doctors whom they thought could help to solve my problems when it was not too late. Now that it is rather late for me to get issues, they still help to console me and to forget about the torturing I have received in life for the sake of having no children.

If any of them needed my advice or financial support, I had been doing my best to satisfy them as good friends. If they were in lack of any of the house utensils, I was always in a position to render help.

I am a Christian but my mother was not. In their days, people worshipped idols more than the true God, because many wonders were always wrought before the gods and it was believed to be nothing but the truth. People contributed much towards buying food to eat before the gods, and this helped to attract the interest of women. Nobody would like to do anything that cannot be benefited to him or her. I dress in a neater way than my mother did. I use English spoons for eating while my mother used native ones made of wood. She used small cooking pots made of clay for eating, but I am now using plates to eat with.

Life has got better in so many ways than the days I was young. Education has brought in more new things than when I was young. At first people depended wholly and entirely on fishing, farming, and at times trading. Now many big companies, shops, fine markets, have been opened for people to work. In days gone by, people never liked staying in zinc houses and they had not sufficient funds to build them. They had a common excuse that zinc houses were always very hot and instead of wasting money on building them, they shared the money to disabled people. Today zinc houses are found at any corner in interior villages because people are made to know the value of such house.

The widow bound by sorcery

I am a free-born daughter of Ndom Ebom, under Uruan District in Uyo Division, but my husband was a native of Ibuno under Eket Division. He was a good native doctor and could perform wonders of all kinds. That made strong men to nickname him 'Ekoriko' (a costly rock). Ekoriko was the grand father's name who was also a strong man in superstition. A costly man of Ekonko was born with only his left leg and that made the people to believe that he was the grand father who had died. According to the people of Ibuno, when his grandfather died his left leg was cut off, so that in his next generation into the world he might also be active as he was before. To retain this man in their family, certain sacrifices were made for the deceased so that he might be born into that very family once more. According to the natives, they said after two years, a child was born with one leg and still in the same family but different father and mother. It was said to be the most wonderful thing in the history of Ibuno. This child grew to be very wicked and believed mainly on nothing but superstition and wonders.

My people were semi-primitive people and they had no idea of keeping birth records rather they counted it according to the number of years that they leave a particular land to fallow before going back to farm. I did not ask my parents about a particular area of bush that was cultivated when I was born but my age group with whom I was fattened are still alive.

I married while I was just a young girl though I did not know how to dress by then. My first menstruation occurred in my husband's house after we had married for three years.

I have really married only once since I was born. When my husband died, I married a certain man in the very village but not long after the man also died. When this incident occurred to me the second time, people thought there might have been something wrong. I started investigating according to the custom and I was made to understand that my former husband pronounced a certain juju on me before he died. He said that after death, any man whom I would marry must die and I must remain to marry his grave in place of him. When I knew of this I was disgusted and decided returning to stay in my father's land.

My husband died about nine years ago. He was a native doctor during his life time. With this he fed well but he made no good thing out of his money because of his wickedness. He was always ready to charm or kill anybody provided he was offered some money.

We were eighteen wives when I married him, I was his seventh wife. Some of the wives were given to him free of charge if after treatment the parents had no money to pay. It was through this method that my husband was able to have a new wife almost every year. And he always said that the number of women he divorced were more than what he had before he died. Many of his wives were offered as sacrifice for his juju that provided him with money. The man was really wicked but my father made me to marry him as he was his friend during the time he was fishing there.

We were given separate houses and all of us respected each other despite age or tribe in which each belonged. We were kind to each other but there was always jealousy among us because my husband loved some of his wives more than others. This was the main thing that brought in jealousy. Secondly, some of my co-wives had no children and there was much jealousy among the two sets of people.

I lived with my father from my youth at Ibuno where he was living and again in my husband's house. My mother as I was told died while I was a child of one year. When my husband died, I came back to live in my father's compound till this present time. I liked living in my husband's house more than here because even though I was not well cared for, yet I was respected as a house wife. But since I came back to live here, people have been worrying me because there is nobody that they could fear me for. As I have no husband, at least I should have got many children but now I am left alone. When the trouble was too much with me at my place, I decided coming to stay here with my son-in-law. And most unfortunately for me my son-in-law died and I had to go back to my father's compound.

I would not describe my life as a happy one because since I was born I have been meeting with many difficulties, even from my youth till this present time. My mother died while I was very small and even in the marriage home I did not enjoy it as other women did. I had five children and all of them died leaving me with only a daughter whose husband died two years ago. My life is indeed a sorrowful one since I grew to full womanhood.

I have been doing some petty trading and a little of farming to feed myself.

As I said before, I had five children and all of them died leaving only one daughter for me. I have seven grandchildren and all of them are children of my daughter whose husband died two years ago. The rest of my children died while they were very young.

Judging from all that has happened to me in life, I should say that since from my youth, I never met with any good things. I was brought up by my father when my mother died, and was given in marriage to a man older than myself, who was also born with wickedness at hand, and this caused my children's death. I was still young when my husband died, but through his wickedness I remained under hardship and never to marry again in life. Considering all of these obstacles, one would see with me that no moment has been experienced which could be described as my happiest time since I was born.

No interesting thing has ever happened to me. Since I grew up to know myself, all things seemed to be against me. I have never had any peace of mind for about a year without any trouble.

In my opinion, I feel it is a bad thing for a woman when the husband has more than one wife because there would be a lot of disputes in the family than it should be when only one wife controls the family. Though there would be many children, yet all of them would be cared for by their respective mothers. Anything that could have been sufficient for only one woman, would have to be shared to many no matter how small it could be.

At the moment, all the kind ones have died and no other person in the family is kind to me. The only person outside my family in whom I can confide is one of our Church elders. He is the only person to whom I always disclose my secrets. He usually gives me good advice to help me in this awful life that I am living. He acts like my own son both in need and also in deeds. I at times go to help his wife in some domestic work that I can do. I even help the wife in farm work and from there I usually have many crops, free of charge from her. Without them it would have been very difficult with me because I have not been having some lands to farm as I had been married, out of my father's compound. It is the custom that if a woman is married out of the father's compound, she must not have a share in anything in the father's compound any more. If she happens to return to the father in case the husband is dead it means she must be buying some lands on which to farm.

My mother as I am told believed in superstition, but I grew to see that if a person devoted his or her interest to doing God's work, he could live in peace and under God's care. Upon all that has happened to me in life, I leave them all to God instead of offering some to unnecessary things with the hope of improving the situation of all that has happened to me in life. In my mother's days, people were forced to believe wholly and entirely in superstition and fear. Now I can see that people are left to do anything they like to each other.

Commentary

This is a story filled with the conflict between two creeds. As a Christian, this widow is impelled to describe traditional practices as 'wicked' or superstitious, but she nevertheless accepts that the 'performing of wonders' takes place.

On the whole, the change of religions is seen as the exchange of a 'protection racket' for a state of total permissiveness.

A deaconess

I was born in one of the villages in Etoi clan under Uyo Province.

The year of the first influenza attack met me while I was a young girl of seven. That was the year my sister who died ran away with me to Ekim Enen, a town in Uruati Clan for protection. The influenza started in Etoi without touching other clans.

My parents gave me to marriage while I was almost eleven years of age.

My present husband is my fourth husband since I was born. My parents first gave me to a man who was staying at Isiet Ekim temporarily as a fisherman for marriage. The marriage lasted for seven years and ended in divorce due to the man's bad behaviour towards me. During the long period of marriage I had no issue for him and this made the marriage to end in divorce. I stayed for a year in my mother's house and was taken to marriage by another man at Esuk Odu, a small island where smugglers usually land their smuggled goods. Here about three-quarters of the inhabitants are wizards and witches. Both men and women alike. My husband was better than some of his brothers as he himself was a native doctor. Many people in his family did not like him as one of their brothers. Fortunately I was able to have one daughter for him but his family people were not happy over the child. When the new-born child was ten days old she fell victim to chickenpox. My husband, being a native doctor, entered a canoe to go and get some herbs in their river bank to mix for the daughter. When he left, two of his brothers who were not happy about his progress went after him without any one's knowledge. Very unfortunately they met my husband alone trying to collect the herbs and there they started beating him and dragged him inside the water. After they had finished their plan they quietly returned to their respective homes. But they were not hidden before the Almighty God who created them. From morning till night I waited for my husband but all in vain. I ran to the relatives and told them how long their brother stayed. Since morning but they made no arrangements to find him out. I ran to the chiefs to lay the complaint and a search had to be conducted, to know the where-abouts of my husband. His corpse was later seen flowing on the river. After his burial my mother took me away with the child of fourteen days I had at hand. And that ended the story of my second marriage.

My third husband came from Ifa but he was a wicked man. We married for three years and with a male child to him. All my co-wives and even my husband were against me. Hatred came from all angles to me without any cause. I decided going to stay in my mother's house peacefully rather than staying among devils without peace. The third marriage ended abruptly.

My present husband was a trader by profession when I married him. He was the first man who brought the first spiritual church in the whole of Etoi Clan. He is still my husband and he proves a very good husband to me. He behaves well with me as a husband in the real sense of it. He is still alive and I still pray God to prolong his life. He has nothing doing at the moment but is one of the elders in the Apostolic Church of Nigeria.

I am the only wife of my husband and I have no co-wives. All those whom he married before had gone and some divorced him. I did not come to meet any of them and I don't know what should have been their feelings if I had come to meet any.

As I have already said, I first married at Isiet Ekim, Esuk and Ifa my home town. I have not lived in other places other than those places that I mentioned.

I like living in this village because it is the place my husband come from. Among all the places I had stayed in those days, I prefer Ifa my present place of living to other places I have mentioned be-cause it is more open. Three-quarters of the villagers are Christians and the practice of witchcraft is not so rampant. People know the value of education and this helps to improve the standard of living among the untrained groups. Everybody is busy working for his daily bread instead of staying idle and causing destruction and all evil practices as most of the people in those places I have mentioned do. In a place like Esuk Odu in Uruan Division, people consider evil practices as parts of their duty. Instead of securing any improvements in them, hardship on their physical outlook will be noticed. Those are some of the reasons why I prefer my present place of living to those where I have already lived.

Even though all my children had died, leaving the one who is doing a degree course abroad, I can describe my life as a happy one because I have been able to marry the type of husband that life requires. Though other members of the family have no love for me, I can say with joy that I have got my husband as my right-hand man in all my affairs. Having seen all that is going on in the present day world, I can boldly describe my life as a happier one than that of my mother. In my mother's days, things were different, and men in general did not value their wives as the present men are doing. Most of these things have helped to make my life a happy one.

When I married my first husband I had nothing doing as I was very small. I started in the third man's house to take farming as a part of my occupation. I started taking farming as my main occupation when I came to marry my present husband because he is a man with so many lands to farm. During my time with my mother I had been doing some craft: things like mats and raffia bags were my occupation. When I started getting my own house, I stopped making them because it takes time to finish one.

I had three children: two males and one female. Two died in the year 1965, leaving me with that one abroad. I have four grandchildren, three from my late daughter and one from the one overseas. All of them are small children.

The happiest time I have ever had in life was when my son was given a scholarship for overseas training, by one Reverend Lydman.

The unhappiest time I have experienced was when I lost two children by death in one year. Though I had been having many unhappiest moments since I grew up to know myself, but the one I have just said was indeed a shock in my life. These two deaths will ever make me very unhappy whenever I remember them. Even though I am at the point of death I can frankly say that nothing can increase my happiness again in life due to this great blow. Even if my son comes back from overseas today he will increase the sorrows because the late ones should have been the people to welcome him and not me an old woman.

The most interesting thing that has happened to me was the time I was annointed a deaconess in the Apostolic Church to which I belong. I am surprised to see myself in this post which I never knew I would be in life. When I had been punishing myself among devils who had no fear of God, I thought that was the end of everything. I never knew I will once marry a Christian who will also help to improve my life also as a good Christian and thereby I became a deaconess.

Comparing my life at the moment with the type of life I was living under a husband of many wives, my life now has changed for the better. There is no jealousy and hatred from co-wives. It is indeed a good thing for a woman when she is the only wife of the husband. It will help the wife to gain full interest and love from the husband. When the husband is interested in the wife and the wife understands all the husband's movements all other things which is required from a husband will move well and take their better stand.

At the moment I have nobody in my former family who has been kindest to me. Those who were kind to me have all died and left me alone. I am alone with my God. Everybody as I can see does not like me. I don't know the main cause why this is so but I seem to see much jealousy among many of them. At times I clash with them in land affairs. As for financial help, my husband is the only person who at times renders help to me when I am in need of any.

I have also been helping my husband as much as I could. I remember giving him some financial help on many occasions but fail to demand it back. There are some years which I usually use about ten pounds or more to buy some lands for farming without demanding a mite back from him. I usually buy some plots of oil palm and hire people to cut them for a year or two without asking him for even one penny. All those are financial help which I have rendered to him for the interest of the whole family.

My life has got much difference from that of my mother in so many ways. In my mother's days I remember as she choose a husband for me to marry and gave a strong order that if I did not marry the man she had chosen I will be forsaken as a daughter. I remember giving my late daughter chance to choose anybody she liked to marry according to the present custom. My first husband did a certain sacrifice to my mother when he came to marry me. It was believed in those days that if a sacrifice was not made to the mother-in-law on behalf of the first daughter who was given to marriage the daughter must get missing at the end of seven days. This I did not do and yet my daughter did not miss at the end of seven days. In my mother's days I don't remember a time when my mother was taken to the hospital when she took ill. Rather a native doctor will be consulted for immediate treatment as her own belief was also in that. Now I can be proud to say with joy that if I am sick today I must treat myself with some simple tablet I know and where I don't see any effect I approach a doctor rather than going to deceive myself with native doctors. Because of civilization I can even see that the number of native doctors now is going down every day. I can say with experience that three-quarters of native doctors whom I know are very deceitful. In my mother's days, it was difficult to convince anybody on what she grew up to see other people do. Now that we have so many ways of proving things, it is rather difficult to blind even an old woman of about ninety years of age in the attempt of playing any ungodly havoc on her. Those are some few points that differentiate my life from that of my mother.

The midwife's tale

I was born in a little rural village in Ifa Ikot Okpon Etoi Clan, Uyo Province.

I am about ninety years of age. When I was born there were no written documents but all I know I can determine my age according to the years of farming. In my village we allow the bush to fallow for seven years before we go back to farm. To the best of my knowledge, I have worked in a particular bush which is allowed to fallow for seven years for thirteen times. Meaning that I have seen ninety Christmasses.

I was married at the age of ten years. In those days in my village husbands were often chosen by the parents for their daughters. Daughters were denied freedom to choose their husbands, hence I was forced by my parents to marry a man more advanced in age than I.

It was not the custom for a woman to marry many husbands except where the husband had died. Even then it was not a common practice. In my case I have only one husband even though I missed him by death many years ago. I felt it improper to serve another husband so I choose to stay and care for my children.

When my husband was alive he was a farmer. He grew such crops that were useful for local consumption. We depended on the crops on his farms. At times he traded on petty crops and tobacco from European firms who were then occupying Ifiayong Beach. I can recall with joy many times when my late husband returned home with some strong drinks and tinned fish from the European firms as mark of good sales.

My husband had a mighty compound with twelve partitions and in each of these partitions a woman and her children lived. All these women were my co-wives.

I cannot say I approve of polygamy because at times we quarrelled and exchanged words such that no right-thinking person would like to use. At times my co-wives used to be kind when we were on good speaking terms. We shared nearly everything in common. But when the offending Adam came, we played the Jew and Samaritans. Where you have one husband with many wives, jealousy is the order of the day. I spent most of my life with my late husband and his wives. Here I found life monotonous and routine.

Even though my life was so monotonous in my husband's house, yet I found pleasure in living with my children in my husband's courts. This I did because of my children. I was afraid to leave them at the mercy of my husband and his wives so I had no idea of living apart from my husband.

I enjoyed everything as I never knew how to change dresses as the modern women do. What every housewife needed in our days from the husband were lands to farm. Immediately that was done the wife had nothing to complain of. I was so much occupied in farm work that I hardly had time to see about other things. I, like my husband, took to trading on sundry farm articles as my hobby.

I have seven children—four daughters and three sons. My first son so well lived and became a village head after his father. I have twenty grandchildren. The young grandchildren of mine often visit me for food.

My happiest time I can remember was when I was confined to the fattening room. Here I was compelled to eat. I was not allowed to walk about or to work in the farm. This was the time when my husband was made to bring to my mother for my well-keeping all her needs. He raised no objection in giving out money to buy anything I required from him.

The unhappiest time in my life was the time my son was taken by death.

The most interesting or important thing I can well remember was when my first son was installed a village head after his father. I say this because it was always unusual to allow a young man to become a village head. Often the oldest person from any family would be allowed to rule after the death of any village head, but this was not the case with my first son. During the installation, many pieces of advice were given to him in my presence. Traditional rites and customary rites were bestowed on him.

For a man to have many wives then was not a bad thing because often more than thirty pieces of land would be cultivated for one man. And if he were to have one wife, most of the work would be left undone. Sometimes there would be scrambling and fighting over the ownership of the pieces of land to be farmed. If a man married one wife he would get a few children and would not be able to cope with the multiple amount of work. In our days, a man's riches were determined by the number of wives he married. Of course I must not also forget about the countless disadvantages brought to the family by the multiplicity of the women. In our days, any man who limited himself to a wife was regarded as a poor and wretched man and his children would not enjoy the fellowship of brethren. There were inter-family wars, for instance, if a man had one wife and a few children, he would be driven away by a thickly populated family.

I am proud to say that my uncle took me as the apple of his eyes. He wouldn't stay in this compound or two without seeing me. He was very fond of advising me on how to marry. He gave me many presents. He shared in every activity in my husband's house.

I had a woman friend to whom I revealed my secrets. She was very fond of keeping secrets to herself. We acted as husband and wife. We always moved hand in glove and my husband and hers knew about our relationship. The villagers nicknamed us twin sisters. When I ran low in funds she would be the only person to render help. When I am out of gear with my husband, she would be the person to restore peace. I remember one day when I was beaten by my husband out of the house, I ran to take shelter in her place, and she gave me a dress and food to eat.

I often sent my children to go and work for her in return for her kindness to me. My husband being very fortunate to get more pieces of land than her husband, allowed some to her even though she was not my co-wife.

I grew to see that my mother in our days never put on gowns; instead, yards of cloth were hung over the shoulder leaving one side of the body bare. With this she could move to anywhere. When the husband died, she was made to stay for months without bath. She was not allowed to comb her hair. The house where the dead person was kept was not swept. All these were done as the last honour to the late husband. This died out in our days. My mother often told me that they were not allowed to cook for the husband during their menstrual periods. She did not enter the husband's house where the juju was kept so that the power of the juju might not get reduced. If a woman disobeyed the order her monthly period will flow for weeks without stopping.

I seem to like the movements of things now. When a woman gave birth to a child in previous days, only leaves of banana or plantain were used as mats for her bed. She was not allowed to take bath until after some days. Wooden basins were used for bathing. Herbs and roots were prepared and kept in a pot and chalk collected from the streams and water was added to this. With this new young babies were baptised every morning with the understanding that this would help them to grow fat and heavy. Today hospitals, clinics and maternity homes have taken the place. Children were not allowed the freedom of seeing or listening to the strangers talk to their parents. If a child stole or committed any crime, he or she often were sold into slavery. Today such things can never happen. With these and many that I do not mention, I find that life is far better than in our days. Of course the modern children seem very proud and will not respect old people; a thing that never happened in our days.

The hunter's wife

I am a free born daughter of Ifa Ikot Ubo, one of the smallest villages in Etoi.

I was a small girl when my senior brother went to the first world war of 1914. I cannot actually know my age, but I was using only two yards of cloth when my brother went and signed to be one of the soldiers.

After my senior brother had left, it was not quite long before I married. I could have stayed longer than that but after my brother had left my father suffered from leprosy and there was no money to give to the man who treated him, and for that reason I was given to a man who paid the debt to the native doctor. The native doctor was given three pounds, and that was all that the man paid on my behalf.

Yes, I have married more than once. I married my first husband for eight years without having any child for him. Through investigations, my parents were made to understand that my husband was practising witchcraft and that was the reason why I was not pregnanted. My parents also discovered that if I continued to marry the man he would kill me. That was the reason my mother went to her friend's husband and collected three pounds for my former husband who released me for my mother.

My last husband died about five years ago. He was a hunter; he was shot to death as he went for hunting expedition. He accompanied his friend for hunting expedition at night and most unfortunately he was shot to death by his friend by mistake because two of them were not going together along the bush.

I have four co-wives plus myself, making five. All of us are still here in the compound since my husband died. Though we were asked to choose any of my husband's relatives for marriage, but none of us accepted to marry anyone because we all have got responsible children who can care for us.

As I was the first wife of my husband, any other wife married into the family was told to respect me. As regards kindness, nobody was forced to be kind to each other but it was always done out of one's free will. All other wives were jealous of me during the time of farming but later on they were fed up because they noticed that in anything they did with me I never retaliated.

I have already made mention of the first husband whom I married and how we ended after my mother discovered the wickedness he was planning on me. Since I was born, I have not lived in any other place than that place and this has been my next place of living.

When I compare certain things in this place to the time I married my former husband, I prefer this place to the former one. When I married my first husband I noticed that people in the compound were not co-operating. This was the reason why the progress of people there was very slow.

There is nothing that makes a woman to be happy in the marriage home more than children. God blessed me by giving me children and there is no other thing that bothered my life. I very much describe my life as a happy one despite the hardship which is almost common in every house of the low-income group like mine. And I do not take hardship as a problem because it is a common sickness to everyone especially in Ibibio land.

According to Ibibio custom, when a woman is newly married, she must be given pieces of lands to farm and through that, every individual will take farming as one of her best handworks. When I say so, I don't refer to the educated women but I mean those who know nothing about the idea of demanding money for food from their husbands. I started life as a farmer even while I was taken to marriage by the first man. Fortunately for me, I came to marry a second husband in a place where there are many fertile lands for farming, and I devoted my interest to it till this present time and it pays me much.

At the moment I have seven children after two have died. I have fourteen grandchildren and five great-grandchildren.

The first happy moment of mine was when my father recovered from leprosy which should have killed the whole of our family. Though many of my parents' properties were sold, yet I was very happy as none of us died as a result of this dangerous attack.

But it was indeed an unhappy time for me when I lost my husband by a fearful death. The death was a shocking death as my husband went out happily for hunting expedition, but he was brought back as a dead body into his house. The death shocked everybody in the village but there was no remedy to get him breath again.

The most interesting thing that happened to me was during the time I brought my first daughter out from the fattening room. I decorated my daughter in the most attractive way and through the way I arranged, many people praised me for all that I did in honouring my daughter.

It is a bad thing these days for a woman when her husband has more than one wife because the cost of living is higher than in days gone by. In days gone by, it was always a good thing for a woman when her husband has more than one wife because there were many pieces of land to farm with. Having many wives helped the husband to have more regular meals than he should have when having only one wife.

My junior brother is the only person in my father's family who is kind to me. I don't mean that he has been giving me presents of money or other things, but he is an influential man to me. In time of trouble he is the only person whom I can tell any of my trouble.

Really I only have my own children as my friends to whom I always confide. I do not rely on anybody because people these days are not trustworthy as some of the women of our days.

Nearly all my children are very helpful to me. They care for my good health and give me some financial help whenever they like. Of course, there is nothing I can do for them again because I am not so active and there is nothing I can do for them any longer. I do not even think that any of my children will be happy to get any present of money from me if even I were to have some.

I am fortunate to have educated children who help to improve my life more than my mother's children were doing to my mother when she was alive.

Yes, life has got better these days than the days when I was young. Many good improvements and all kinds of amenities that people are now enjoying were not in operation in olden days.

The pawned daughter

I was born at Isiet Ekim, a village in Uyo Division.

I don't know my exact age as my parents had no idea of keeping such records.

I was given in marriage at the age of seven according to my late mother. According to my mother, I was pledged to a native doctor during the first attack of influenza in the year 1926. After my mother had been cured, there was no money to give to the doctor. People said the doctor was prepared to call some evil spirits to come and kill my mother if they refused paying him. On hearing this, my people were afraid and they decided to give me to the doctor until twenty manillas (worth five shillings) were paid to him as promised. I was there in the man's house as a house maid to one of the doctor's wives until I was mature enough to live in a separate room as one of the doctor's wives as my people still had no five shillings to come and redeem me.

I have been married twice since I was born. After my first husband had died, I was taken in marriage by one of his sons. Since his death about seven years ago, I decided not to marry again until the call of God comes to me.

None of my husbands is alive. They were all native doctors during their days.

We were altogether seven wives to my first husband, and all of us were engaged by members of the family after his death. Some of the wives respected me when I became officially married to the doctor. They were at the same time happy to get me in their midst as one of the wives and no more house maid. They were kind to me at first, but after a few years they began to hate me as they thought their husband was more interested in me as a new person than any of them. Jealousy started in full swing against me when they started seeing some improvements in me. Of course, the improvements were temporary and within a very short time things were automatically changed.

I have been living in this same place since I was married by my late husband. I have not lived anywhere else other than here since I grew up to full womanhood. I like living here because all my three sons are also having their houses here on the father's land.

I can describe my life as a happy one because in my early days there was not much civilization as it is today. In those days, men were highly respected when they married as many wives as they could. I was happy to belong to a family manned by an able man such as my husband was.

I spent most of my life as a farmer, but now I am unable to farm to a large scale because I am fairly old.

I have five children and eighteen grandchildren after three had died.

The happiest time in my life was when my two daughters got married and all of them gave issues to their respective husbands during my life time. This assured me that any time I die I shall have many grandchildren to give me the last honour as I did to my mother.

My unhappiest time was the year my first daughter died in the fattening room. That was indeed the greatest blow to me since I was born. The happening was very unique and ominous to the affected family.

It was the custom that whenever a young woman would be delivered of her first son, the mother had to equip her house with all domestic requirements. My mother played her part very well. I am very proud of those gifts and I am preserving them.

In my opinion I think it is a good thing for a woman when the husband is a polygamist. There will be many women to take care of the husband. Women will not be oppressed by farm work as should be on one woman. Many wives help to increase the number of children in the family instead of expecting more from one woman alone.

My grandmother had been kindest to me. This woman died about ten years ago and since then I have been left alone. There is no one who has interest in me. Even my brothers whom we all come from the same womb are very unkind to me.

I have no good friend at the moment whom I can confide in. All those I had in olden days had died. They were indeed good friends to me as I was to them. Since they left I have not been able to get even one of such friends. Especially most of my age groups in this village belong to different societies which I had already neglected. Some of these ungodly societies are: Ebre, Idiong, Ndem and many others. I was at first one of the members in some of these societies, but my daughter converted me into the Roman Catholic Church to which they belong. Since then I have not shared anything in common with my mates who are still in these societies. Also, they don't co-operate with me as they did at the time we all were together. It is difficult for me to associate with any average person who is not my age. That is why I choose to stay alone instead of pleasing myself and then displease my daughters who take care of me now.

Those friends whom I had in the old days were very good to me as indeed I was to them. During the time of farming such as we are having now, many of them who had less to do came to stay with me about three or four days to help me in farm work. I had also been asking my own children to go and help them in their job as well. I had in those days been helping them financially. Indeed, I helped most of them in the way I could. Not all my friends were the same: I had some who were very deceitful and those who were very trustworthy. In any case I tried as I could to show my great interest and kindness to those who deserved them.

My life has now been quite different from that of my mother in so many ways. My mother was older than myself, but I have seen many more strange things than she did.

In days gone by, I grew up to see how my mother had been rubbing herself with scarlet substance produced from red iron wood after her bath. They had been doing this after a hard day's work, and this was believed to have kept their skins smooth. Girls of those days were using headties around their neck. Something called scabies also attacked children during their younger days. If you happen to observe some of the old women now, you will surely see some scars all over.

Another marked difference is in connection with the ways my mother and her parents observed some rites in order to retain the memory of any member of the family who might have died. The observance featured the erection of a stump in a corner of one of the rooms in the compound, about two feet high. A round hole was made on top of the stump. It was then the belief that the dead also required their own share of whatever the living ate, especially palm wine. To satisfy this condition, some quantity of palm wine was generally poured on the stump of the dead. The mere fact that the wine dried up immediately showed the willingness of the dead to drink the share given him. The number of such stumps showed the number of the dead who were expected to share in it.

There was also a cultural society into which men only were initiated. It was known as 'Ndok'. Masquerade display marked the arrival of the season which came every other year. The masquerader applied some pipe covered at one end with the soft membranous wing of a bat to his lips. This changed the voice to something hoarse. Moonlight was the most favourable time for them. Women could only listen to the singing and funny stories produced by the masqueraders from behind their yards. On the last day of the year when the season was to be ended, certain traditional rites were observed in every family. On the last day, the initiated men would go to sacrifice for the dead men on their graves. The requirements included a cock, a yam, and some herbs. A small tent was built near the grave with mats. The head of the cock was cut and the blood sprinkled around the small tent and the yam cut in pieces and left there around the grave. The body of the fowl was taken home and eaten by all members of the family.

At midnight on December 31st, both the end of the year and the termination of 'Ndok' season were marked by gun shots, throwing of smouldering wood all over the place and shooting of arrows carrying fire. These were accompanied by indiscriminate shouting from all houses asking the old year to disappear with all its attendant evils and ill luck. The new year was heralded in the following day with many plays and dances. Around the village the 'Ekpe' masquerade would dance picking from street to street all the pieces of wood thrown away the previous night.

Life has completely changed and it is in my opinion better than the days I was born.

A fortunate woman

I was born in a little village in Ifa Atoi in Uyo Division of Eastern Nigeria, which is about six miles from the Uyo-Oron road. It is a big undeveloped village with winding paths running through it. Until recently there was no permanent building of any kind, but the people had to be contented with mud and wattle buildings with thatched roofs.

I am roughly eighty-one years of age. In those days there was no birth registry in this area and there were only very few people who could write, but my father was not one of those who could keep my birth record. There was, however, a method through which the people calculated their ages. In this village, we always leave a piece of land to return to fallow for about nine years before going back to farm on that special area. To the best of my knowledge, I have farmed on a special area of land nine times. That means I have done nine times nine years, and I must be about eighty-one years or a little over that.

In our days, there was no free choice of husband or wife by the couples concerned. Marriage between two couples was often arranged by the parents of the couples concerned. There was a little chance given to the male folk but there was no choice for the girls, so I was given over by my father to a man well over or double my age when I was doing my seed round on a special area of farm land, so I must have been about eighteen years of age when I was given over. The question of love before marriage was completely out of place in my days and refusal of a girl to marry a man chosen for her by her father was regarded as a defiance of authority and after carried a heavy and severe punishment of being disowned by the parents and driven out of the compound, and only few girls would live to bear such shame.

Divorce could never be thought of in my days. The wife was

regarded as the life-long property of the husband. When once a girl was married, she was married and would live in her husband's compound until death did them separate. Even if the husband died, it was not usual to have a woman leaving the compound of the husband unless she had no child for the man. Where the woman had children for the man, she had to stay with her children to bring them up. Marrying a dead man's wife was often looked down upon, and so even if the woman should want to go out to marry, nobody would like to marry her. Sometimes young girls had to go without children for life because their husband died not long after their marriage. As there was no choice of husband by the girls, it was not unusual to find a girl of, say, twelve being given over to a man of over fifty who would die before the girl was ready for the husband to put to family way. This brings us to another important point: fattening. A girl after marriage had to be circumcised and then kept in the fattening room for at least three years before she would be given over to the husband. The end of the fattening period was often marked with celebration and feeding of the whole village by the father of the girl as everybody in the village would be feeding fat on him. People who did not fatten their daughter were often disgraced publicly for being tight-fisted and often called, 'tortoise hands'. Such people were few in those days.

As stated already, I was given over to a man double my age. We lived together happily for many years and I gave him nine children three of whom died before my husband. My husband grew to be very old and could not go out for anything again but only to sit out each day of the week in his sitting room for guests who would come to seek his wisdom on certain issues of the village. In spite of his age, he always gave out what was considered to be the best advice. One day, he called me and told me that he wanted to go a long journey to lands unknown to him. I did not understand him at first, and I was wondering how he would manage to travel when he could no longer walk a distance. While still trying to know what he meant by this, my husband commanded me to give him water to bathe and also food to eat. These I did at his command and after devouring the food with great appetite, he lay down and died. This happened about ten years ago and I have since been living with my children to marry them as we always say.

Farming has always been regarded as the main occupation of this village and whatever other work a man did, he had to own a few plots of farm land each year for his daily supply of foodstuffs. Secondly, the wealth of a man was not so much reckoned on how much money he had but on how many pieces of farm land he had in a year. A man who had less than twenty plots in one year was regarded as a poor man. My husband looked down upon anybody who could not boast of yams in his barn to the tune of one thousand stands during harvest. He would therefore do everything within his power to see that he cultivated between thirty and forty plots each year and up to his death he was very much interested in farm work and often encouraged his sons by helping them to tie up the yams in the barn during the harvest.

Farming in the primitive way entails much labour, and so it was not unusual to find a man marrying up to twenty wives for the sake of farming. My husband had sixteen wives, six of whom died before my husband. Three of the remaining ten have since died and seven of us are still living in my dead husband's compound. My husband had thirty-nine children left at his death—twenty-five males and fourteen females. The fourteen females all got married before my husband died, but six of them are now dead. Ten of the twenty-five sons died and only fifteen of them are now living in the compound. They have all married and built their own houses within their father's compound. If any son should leave his father's compound to live anywhere else, he would be considered a prodigal son, so you have people of the same family living close together.

My father was a very rich and influential man in the village and was highly respected. He was a man who would not forgive anybody who trampled upon his right or the right of his children. This influence of my father transferred much respect to us so that though I became the seventh wife of my husband, I was always looked upon as the head of my husband's house. The only reason of this being that I gave birth to the first son my husband had and, secondly, they feared my father rather than me. At my husband's death, my son became the head of the family, thus giving me a respectful position among the women.

In spite of squabbles, which are never lacking among women, we all used things we had in common. We were always very kind to each other and anything happening to one person was regarded as happening to all of us, and everyone of us would share the burden equally. Any woman who showed a sign of unkindness to others would be called before my husband to explain herself and if a good satisfactory reason was given, she would be asked to buy a goat or a fowl to prepare a meal and appease others. All our children often ate from common plates.

The life of having co-wives is a jealous life. The wives who had male children were often treated with special preference, so I fell into this group. Other women, especially the first six wives of my husband, were really jealous of me for having this position. This did not get serious because my husband would not stand for any talk touching any of his sons.

When I was a girl of about nine I went out to live with one uncle of mine for a very short period. My uncle was a produce buyer at Uyo, which is the only town near us. Apart from my not liking to live at Uyo because of the quickness and busy life of the town, I did not very much like to leave my mother for a long time. Since I grew up to marry my late husband I do not remember sleeping away from his compound except when my father died when I went to stay in our compound for a short time until my father's memorial service was held, after about three weeks of his death. He was until his death a full member of the Church, and so his memorial service had to be held after such a short spell of time.

I was born here, I grew up here, and I am completely used to this village. I doubt if I would bear to live outside my village for a while. I do not know what attractions there are in other places and so I consider my home to be the best.

Indeed, I have always considered myself the luckiest of women. I was born of rich family and had everything I needed, from wealth to respect. When I got married I thought I would be treated as the last among equals but found myself becoming the head of the family. I went beyond six other wives only because I happened to give birth to the man's first son. I sometimes asked why it is that I should give birth to the first son of a man who had married for over ten years before I got into his life and came to a conclusion that God had made me to be great from the cradle to the grave. Only very few women have been blessed with such good fortunes as I have had in my life. My sons have all grown up to become rich and love me. With this I am confident that I shall have all the funeral rites when I die.

In our days, women were considered completely dependent on their fathers and husbands, and so there was no need for giving an occupation to the women. I have however been taking up petty farming as the main occupation I have had for life. At this age, I do not think I shall have a second occupation before I die in a few years' time.

I gave birth to nine children but three died, remaining six children. My first son has six children yet, my second son four. Other sons have three, three and two. My daughter has already given birth to the fifth child. I have a total of thirty children and grandchildren.

As I have already stated, I have no time in my life which I should consider as an unhappy one. But I have always looked upon the day when my daughter's fattening ceremony was held as my happiest moment. This placed me on equal footing with all other respected women in the village as a woman whose daughter was fattened before being given over to marriage. The next moment of my life I should consider as very important is when I had my first grandchild. Grandchildren are the happiness of their grandmothers, especially when the woman becomes old. The grandchildren will sit round her, to listen to her bed-time stories. They will do simple jobs as fetching water, fetching firewood and sweeping for their grandmother.

The loss of children or friend close to one has always been a sad moment for one anywhere in the world. The loss of my three children has always come to me as the greatest loss I have suffered in my life. The moments of the great loss have always been considered the unhappiest moments of my life. But I have been brought up to believe that death is for everybody. Deaths have occurred so often that I cease to think of my loss as a hard luck. Secondly, I know that one day I shall have to leave this world through death. My other endowments have cancelled out my unhappy moments so I cease to think of them seriously.

Though my husband was double my age when I married to him, I have always considered the opportunity I had to get married as the most important moment of my life. In our part of the world there is almost an overproduction of women and only the lucky and very beautiful girls get married. I was not beautiful at youth but was endowed with a disciplined mind which I had from my father and mother. One should not fail to see why I consider my marriage to a very wealthy man with at least forty plots of land to farm every year, as the most interesting moment of my life. Then came the moment I, through giving birth to my husband's first son, was proclaimed the head of my husband's family. These to a woman would delight her.

Having co-wives would be good at times and be bad at other times. As already expressed, the main reason for a man marrying many wives was not so much for the sake of marrying as the need for the wives. There was never a year when my husband has less than forty plots of farm land. There were other years when he had up to seventy and this would mean much work for the women who would be responsible for the planting of all the crops. The men would only clear the bush, set fire to them when dried, dig the yam holes for the women, look after the yam tendrils and of course help in the harvest of the yams. All other work in the farm would be done by the women. Unless a man had many wives, he would not be able to cope up with the amount of work he had to do in a year. Extended family life has always been the African way of life and so the co-wives would act as your immediate neighbours and friends. The only thing in having co-wives is the fact that your husband will not have much time for any one woman. He has to share his love between the lot of wives and this has always led to grumbling or even open quarrels among the wives as one woman would be accusing the other of trying to monopolize their husband by sleeping in his house for more than a night when all others have not taken their turns. This happened only when the men concerned did not know how to plan. In my husband's case, each of us had only a right to sleep with my husband for one month, and everybody had to keep to the order in which she had to go in. The life of having co-wives is however full of jealousies.

In our family we were all brought up to believe in mutual help. This makes it difficult for me to say exactly which member of my family has been kindest to me, as we believed that what happens to the eyes affects the nose, and would run to rescue anybody who falls a victim of any mishap. But I cannot place the kindness of other people on the same level with that of my mother. I shall never forget her regular visits to me with a small plate or dish full of something to eat until her death five years ago. My father ws equally kind to me but he said I was the seed of the African oil bean which could fall to anywhere during explosion, so he attached more importance to the males who were called the owners of my father's compound.

Right from my youth, I had a friend who was said to be of my age group. We grew up together and entered the fattening room the same year. Fortunately for us, we got married to two great friends and the relationship between our husbands which was cordial helped to cement our long-established friendship. She told me every bit of her business and none of my own has been hidden from her. She keeps what we call secret secret and of course has very few friends.

Up to the age we are now, she has never let me down and I have never let her down too.

She works in my farms with me after which we both go to work in hers, or vice versa. Whenever she is in want—this rarely happens—I always rush to help her and she does likewise to me. At old age as I am, I still find some time to have a chat with her and seek her wisdom and advice on matters affecting me, and she does same when she has same difficulty. We live in mutual help and understanding and, of course, if our help were to be one-sided our friendship would soon land on the rocks. I do everything to help her in her work, especially farm work.

Things are different in our days than they were in mother's days. Civilization has brought in many changes into our lives now. So that we do not have to live in fear and superstition. There were so many things in which my mother believed which I have discovered to be false; for example, our village always set aside one day in a week as the day when the god of water would come out to take bath and so nobody went to the spring on such days. On such days, the women would not drink palm wine, otherwise the wine palm tree would cease to contain any more wine. All the men would go to the village hall on such days to drink all the palm wine tapped in the whole village without a drop being sold. Such beliefs are now dying out.

There are also many changes for both the worse and the better life since my mother's days. There is no more respect for the elders from the young ones. Everybody is equal now. Both father, mother and children eat from a common plate where in my mother's days the women had to eat separately from the men and only male children would ever dream of eating with their fathers. The stopping of slave trade has tended to make children unruly as they have nothing to fear as against the fear of being sold which the children had in those days. The children nowadays, even the old people, are falling into moral decay and this has brought about many fatherless children.

The oldest inhabitant

I was born in a village called Use Offot in Uyo Division of the Old Calabar Province.

When I was born there was not a single person who could write nor read hence my age is quite uncertain, but I can boldly say that in Offot Clan presently I am the oldest person. I was a grown-up girl when the first European visited my grandfather, the late Ebot-Akpan-Ebot. One can then fancy my age. I was a matured girl when there was no road in the whole clan area: I mean motor roads as we have them now. My eyes have seen changes though I cannot make right from wrong now. I am in brief about one hundred years old.

Early marriage was esteemed a necessity in those days, hence my late father gave me in marriage when I was only ten years of age. Nevertheless, my first husband was very dear to me and was a palm wine tapper who died when I was seventeen years in his house. After his death I took a relation of his in marriage whom I gave three daughters plus the six sons and two daughters my former husband had from my early conceptions.

To my discredit, my second and last husband died when I had already become worn out and he too was sufficiently old. I wish I had died with him.

My first husband was a hunter and he had one of the most powerful hounds in the whole of this area. I always enjoyed the meat and if any other women ever enjoyed her husband by that time, I was the only one. We were rich, happy, and lived peacefully.

I had seven co-wives as wealth of the past was estimated on the number of wives a man could marry. This was the main reason I encouraged my two late husbands to endeavour to marry as many wives as possible.

With my first husband, I had practically no difficulty as I was the first wife, and he took me as his mother. My co-wives were living by my dictations so that when I passed orders I had none to reject them. They respected me and spoke kindly to me and our husband. But when my turn came to receive commands from the senior wife of my second husband I was somehow a difficult woman. One of the causes was that my second husband inclined to love me more than his other three wives, and they took umbrage upon me because of my beauty.

In our days, girls in particular seldom travelled abroad. So I cannot boast of knowing any other place apart from my village and the surrounding villages not more than six miles in radius.

Home is the best place for everyone and in my own case, I never spelt the mood of life elsewhere as I was married in the very village of my birth. I like living in Use Offot because we have water, plenty of food, the staple one being cassava.

My life at the beginning was in fact a very happy one, particularly when my first husband was alive and when I was in my first teens and even up to my late thirties. But when my first husband died, and two of my children followed, the tide changed. I began to swallow the bitter pills. Worse still when my second husband died, my co-wives nicknamed me as they liked. In that state, all my sons died one after the other. I am now left with only three daughters and countless grandchildren. I was happy a bit at first but, as I am drawn nearer my grave, life becomes more bitter than I can bear.

As for my daily work, I did the simple farming and trading as those were the natural ways of maintaining life.

I had twelve children and most died leaving me with only three. I have about twenty grandchildren both from those who died and also from those remaining ones.

The happiest time of my life was the time I was in the fattening room. My husband brought all that money could buy and my father did all he could to make me happy and fat as I was his first daughter. On a fixed day, we the fattening girls, would go to the market, so that our parents might be mocked at should any one among the girls fail to be very fat. We walked in the state of nature in the market and our proposed husbands carried us on their shoulders round the market.

I say this with tears that the burial of my last son, Awana, at the age of twenty-three, when I was unable to use my limbs again, created the most unhappy period of my life even up to this day.

Several interesting things happened to me during my stay in this world but the one I will state here occurred when I was fifty. In the 'Ebre' society to which I belong, no thief has ever been admitted to dance or even to sing. But one day as we staged our play, a notorious thief came in and danced. As the leader of that particular society, I dragged the thief out and disgraced her. Finally, all of us were arrested by the police who treated us mercilessly simply because we treated the thief in the way we liked due to her disobedience. Each and every one of us was arrested and that was my first time of standing trial in the court. Though as a leader, I was heavily fined, the rogue died as a result of our beating. I considered that to be the most astonishing thing that happened to me because I never knew one could be severely dealt with, simply because of the punishment given to a fellow-woman who broke the order of the society.

Though in those days, those who married many wives were often regarded the most richest men but there are many evils that could come into the marriage home as a result of having more than one wife. When I first married my former husband things moved well and straightforward with me in the marriage home, but when strange faces started coming into the family, things got changed automatically. Children started dying without serious sickness. When these women were married in, though they never expressed their bad feelings, many of them often tried all that they could to bring in confusion between me and my husband. They did all they could to turn my husband's eyes away from my children, but as I was a daughter of a native doctor, they never succeeded in all their attempts.

One friend I had outside my family was one Umo Ille. During our girlhood, we seldom keep our secrets from each other. It was she who approved my first husband, having rejected many suitors. I had been doing all that I could to assist her in anything of hers as she did with me. I did all that she needed of me provided it was within my power to do.

It is not wise to blow one's own trumpet. I feel if she were here she could have been the only person to remark that I, too, did help her. I remembered spending one thousand manillas for her rescue when she had a serious case with a certain man. Up till the present moment, I have not demanded it back from her.

In my mother's days, there was no main roads, rather bush tracks were used. People had no means of going faster to any place desired as I can now see. My mother lived under superstition and fear. In her days, people were often killed like fowls immediately any offence was committed.

My life, however, is worse than hers, having buried all my sons and husbands. One can clearly see the bitter life I am now suffering.

Commentary

The general opinion of this woman's clan is that she is about one hundred and thirty years old, but this is hardly borne out by her appearance.

This tale is chiefly interesting for the illustration of the contrast between traditional and colonial justice. In the customary code, the punishment for theft was to be sent to coventry, but if the thief ignores this injunction, the punishment could amount to lynching, according to the anger aroused. The astonishment of the women's society leader is roughly equivalent to that of a magistrate jailed for carrying out his duties.

A conservative

I was born at Mbak, a village in Etoi Clan under Uyo Province.

I can count my age to be about sixty years. My age group have all died. I was about ten years at the time Chief Umo Etok Eyen disappeared at Inyang Idem on hunting expedition. I married during the year the incident occurred to Umo at our stream and I was about eleven years of age. In those days we did not believe in moving about: we settled down for better or for worse.

I have married once since I was born. My husband is still alive and in fact he is even stronger than I. Men refuse to grow old as we do. He is a petty trader. He trades on tobacco and with this he is able to earn a living.

My husband married eight wives, and that was the order of the day in those days. I was the first no doubt, three are dead so only five are now left. I have been living happily and sisterly with my co-wives. I can boast that since these women were married by my husband, we have never had any serious quarrelling because as a senior and eldest wife among them, I am always respected. When some of my co-wives died, I was so much worried and sad about their death. Because since they came into the family, jealousy has never crept into our midst.

It was the custom that, when a woman gave birth to the first child, she must be invited by relatives to come and stay for a week or two. This helped to reduce some responsibilities from the mother. In my own case, I remembered staying in five houses for some months before I was sent back to my mother. Those women I stayed with were my aunts and one of them was my husband's mother. Apart from my husband's house, there is no other place I have stayed other than those I have mentioned. This type of visit was also a mark of kindness to the persons concerned, mostly the mother and the child.

I am too old to change my residence. Perhaps you feel I would like to leave the village for the urban area. No, I am happy to be here.

My life has been a happy one with my husband and children. Since my youth, I have always been happy. I was the last child in my family and in fact I was so much cared for that some of my brothers and sisters were jealous of me. When I got married, there was no break in my happiness because my husband loved me. Although life has its ups and downs, but I seem to see that my happy moments outweigh unhappy moments.

Though I am fast running to seed, I am still active. My occupation is trade. I trade mostly in fish and in fact that has helped me a lot in schooling my children. I have been in the trade for more than thirty years. I always feel unhappy if I don't go to market a day unless I am not sound in health.

I have ten children. Seven sons and three daughters. My first daughter is married with six children. My first son is also a trader with many children as well. My second daughter was married about twelve years ago and the husband has sent her back to school. She hopes to finish the course end of this year. I have about fifteen grandchildren at the moment.

My happiest moment in life was the time I gave birth to my first son. I married my husband for eight years, we did not get any child. When I was even ready to divorce him, conception took place.

The saddest time in my life was the time I remained in my husband's house for many years without a child. This was the time I received headache from any of my husband's relatives coming unto the compound. I had no rest in mind, and I was accused of being the worst person yet on earth. Though my husband was still interested in me, yet I was not allowed to have any rest from his relatives. When God gave me my first child I regarded the past years as the most unhappiest time when I remembered all disturbances I had from my husband's relatives.

The most interesting thing that happened to me was the time I was appointed as one of the elder women to represent our dancing group in Uyo during the time of election. I was dressed with costly beads by the village heads in Etoi Clan to represent the whole women for them. Though this was done for the interest of the whole village, yet it was a glory to me because I was not the only old woman then.

In my days it was a good thing for a woman when her husband married many wives. One wife in those days could not be able to do much work in the farm as could be done by many wives. Many wives helped to feed the husband because we had to share the cooking of his meat among ourselves. Many wives helped to increase the number of children in the family than one wife could do.

The member in the family which is kindest to me is my sister-in-law. She is quite a good woman to me.

I have no good friends outside my family in whom I can confide. The only person I have is my sister-in-law. She usually helps me in domestic affairs and also in financial affairs. I also help her in the way I could but as my sister-in-law she is expected to do the greatest part for me as a brother's wife and a senior person for that matter.

Life now is different from that which my mother experienced in many ways. A person can travel to any place without any fear. In my mother's days there was no bicycles and they travelled on bush tracks to distant places. The standard of living has risen considerably and everybody enjoys a mild standard of living. Subsistence economy was prevalent then. People died in hundreds because there was no medical care and treatment. Nowadays the death toll is greatly reduced. I wear good and clean clothes now whereas my mother hardly wore something better than a rag.

Life is vast and difficult now. When I was young, with two pence a whole family could feed for a week. But now, two pence is no money. When I was young, the moral standard of young people was really high but now the moral standard has fallen to the dust. I can boast that my husband was the first person with whom I had my first sexual intercourse. In my days, children were always honest. But now honesty has been thrown to the air and life becomes worse. The good thing in life this time is that the modern civilization has brought in education to change most of the things. The poor have no chance nowadays, whereas in my days the poor were able to feed and clothe cheaply. People were less corrupt than they are now. It's this corruption that has plunged the present generation into this chaos.

Commentary

This wife demonstrates clearly the uneasy situation of the childless woman. During the eight years she was without child, she was continually under suspicion, since such women are invariably thought to be plotting against relatives who are already mothers.

Although she is appreciative of material progress, she shows a deep ethical conservatism and nostalgia for the higher moral standards of her youth.

The twin who survived

I was born at James Town, one of the 'Greek' in Oron. According to some old men in Oron, they told me that my parents were not born in James Town rather they came from Greek Town in Calabar. It happened that in those days, twin mothers were often kept in isolation or killed. My mother having conceived during that time, gave birth to twin babies and one died, leaving me alone. The people of Greek Town tortured my mother in the way they could and at last she was killed. My mother also had no influential man behind her and nobody had any sympathy on the woman. After the woman had been buried they carried me to where they buried my mother and there they left me on my mother's grave and went away.

As I was told, a good Samaritan who stayed at Greek Town went to pluck some cassava in her farm. Suddenly, she heard a child crying inside the bush. Having gone in to see what the mother did in the bush with a small child, the woman saw the child lying on a grave. She raised an alarm and later ran and picked up the child.

The story said that when the child was brought into the village, she was driven away by the chiefs of the village and she later ran away with the child to James Town where she came from. This woman had stayed with her husband for many years without any child. When she picked me up on my mother's grave she was overwhelmed with joy and adopted me as her own daughter. She nursed me until I grew up. I grew up in the same house without knowing that she was not my real mother. There in the family, people loved me more than the others, but when my adopted parents died, things started to change.

Hatred came from all angles and they started giving me nicknames until later they revealed to me that I was not the real daughter of my pretended mother. It was too late for me to go and ask the family I came from at Greek Town, rather I chose to stay by the name of the woman who nursed me from youth.

I cannot tell my age because nobody took record of my birth. My adopted mother was not so settled in mind as to have kept such records. My adopted mother never allowed me to marry early because she employed me to serve her mainly on domestic affairs as she had no other person in the house. I had already a bust when I married.

I have only married once since I was born, but although my husband is still alive yet he lives in another village with one of his other wives. That wife was married to him by his mother while he was a boy. The wife never wanted the husband to marry any other woman except her. Unfortunately for her, the husband came and married me and she later got offended and deserted the husband for three years.

After we had married for five years, my husband decided to go and stay with the wife in his father-in-law's compound so that she might know really that he has no interest again for me his newly-married wife. This thing occurred while I was very young and since that time I have had no interest in another man. I am staying here with my son and he gives me help as he could.

My husband was a born fisherman but now I have no idea of his job again.

As I said before, we were two wives when I was married by the man. His first wife never wanted him to marry another woman and this made her to run away immediately I was married. Though people have different customs according to the type of place they come from, yet the way my co-wife acted was very strange to me, but as I had nobody behind me nobody blamed my husband for having left the house for me. At last, I was made to understand that the woman ran away from the house because she was made to understand how I was brought to Oron and she thought she could eventually deliver twins if she shared her husband with me. (She was not ever happy to see me, nor would she share one husband with me.)

Where I am living is where I like best since my children are also staying here.

Though my life was a happy one when I grew up to know my mother, yet the death of my mother made all things to get different shape. When my adopted parents were alive, I equally enjoyed life and I never dreamed of having any bitterness in life. When these two deaths occurred, people started hating me without any cause. My husband, who could have become my mother, father, brother and at the same time a husband to me, was misled by his senior wife and I became stranded in life till now. Fortunately I started experiencing some good changes when my children grew up.

The main occupation of this place is trading and I started this by going to market daily with my late mother until I was up to the age of selling my own wares by myself. As my mother was a fish seller, she taught me how to sell fish until finally she assisted me to buy my own canoe and hired some active men to paddle it for me. From this I could clothe myself and was able to educate my children to what they are today.

I have two sons with eleven grandchildren.

The happiest time in my life was during the time I married a wife for my first son. I did my best as a woman and made my husband feel that even though he neglected me, I could still live. I again made my junior son to become a full member of the 'Ekpe' society without minding how costly it was. I did all these things in one week and made the people of Oron feel that I could still live without a husband.

When my husband ran away from me, I was very sad within myself, but I never knew that God wanted to set me as an example to most of the people who hated me after my mother's death. That was the unhappiest time I had experienced after the death of my adopted mother.

The most interesting thing that happened to me was during the time I was exposed out of the fattening room. I was well decorated with costly beads, gold and costly apparels. Before I was brought outside, my mother had arranged everything that a woman needed before she started life for me. Though I was not married by then, yet she did all that as a sort of honour to me and to reveal her love towards me, as the only child she had. A mighty wooden box, a she-goat, cooking utensils and other eatable things were arranged in order of greatness before I came out. A small girl of about five years of age also sitting beside those things so that even though I was exposed from the fattening room, I was not allowed to do any other thing than eating. The duty of the girl was to run all errands for me. When all these things were presented by my mother, my father added forty manillas so that I could use that to start trading at my convenience. That was the most interesting thing that happened to me because ever in the history of my people; nobody had ever arranged such for her daughter, particularly an unmarried girl as I was.

For myself, I would say that it is a good thing for a woman when the husband has more than one wife because the wife would have other co-wives to feed the husband in case the senior wife is away. If the first wife is not fortunate to bear men-children, the husband would not be offended with her often as he should because he knows that other wives are still increasing the family for him. A polygamous family is always very interesting to watch, particularly during the time of quarrelling. This period is always interesting because all that had been done in secret will be said outside and from there one could know who is the best wife of the husband.

I have already said that after my mother's death nobody in the family regarded me as anything. Many nicknames were given to me and I was neglected. It was this time that I understood that I was only an adopted daughter in the family and nothing more than that.

When my mother was alive I had many friends outside my family in whom I could confide. When my mother died, those friends were not trustworthy any more. I also became uninterested in them. They often made me to clash with other friends by telling them false stories against me. Nevertheless, they had been helping me both in domestic affairs and in farm work. They regarded my late mother equally as their own mother. I had nothing to complain of them nor did any of them prove fed up with my manners. I had also been trying my best to help them until such a time I discovered that they were trying to create heavy troubles for me.

I should say that my life is almost the same as that of my mother because my mother was brought up by the early missionaries who helped to teach her the way that a woman could behave both for her interest and for the interest of her fellow beings. The only different thing I can see being changed from my mother is the changes that people have brought in to enlighten the country as a whole. If I had known that things would be as difficult as it is at the moment, with the little qualification I had, I could have been working for those missionaries while things were not as clear as this. On those days, those who were fortunate to read up to standard four, as it was then called, were often enabled to choose any branch of work they would like to do. This could really prove that my mother was dwelling under the primitive tradition else she could have encouraged me to do that job and things could not have been what they are to me now. Though much more struggling, I have been able to earn a living, yet, if I had accepted the share that had been given to me, I could have been in a better post today and perhaps one of my sons could have been given adequate education.

Even though I have been able to produce what I can eat, yet I cannot consider to have got a better life now than the days I was young. When I was young, I lived under my mother's care, and she had never complained of getting tired of me. Since I left her house to the marriage home, I started seeing differences every day and this really proves that life has got worse with me than the days I was young.

Commentary

On the map Greek Town is usually shown as Creek Town, but since the latter could logically be the name of any town in the Delta, one might well accept the name given by this 'twin woman', particularly as she uses it to distinguish nationality. There is no reason why the inhabitants of this area should not include Greek traders among their ancestors.

This woman is typical of her generation in regarding the Mission as the organ of social mobility. Though it is highly probable that without her Mission background, the kind foster-mother would never have summoned the courage to rescue a rejected twin, yet the adopted daughter regrets that she did not enjoy the further advantage of Mission contact, namely advancement in her career.

The blind man's wife

I am a native of Mbak Akpan Ekpenyong, one of the smallest villages in Etoi under Uyo Province. In olden days some of the smallest villages were named for any of the oldest chiefs of that village who ruled the village peacefully and who was very sympathetic in his ways. That was the reason why this part of Mbak was called or addressed to our late chief Akpan Ekpenyong.

In my days birth dates were calculated according to the number of times people planted on a particular bush that fallowed for seven years. That was how my age was counted, but when much time had passed they forgot about the particular bush-land that was planted when I was born and forgot also about any big event that took place that year.

In those days parents often gave their daughters for marriage at their early age. That was the time I was forced by my parents to marry a man who was even older than my father himself. Of course, it was not my husband who negotiated to marry me, but my mother-in-law, who was interested in the way I had been helping my mother and that feelings moved her to come and marry me to her son who had got four wives already.

My present husband is my fourth husband since I was born. My first husband married me for only five years and died. According to our custom then, they handed me to his junior brother for marriage. I married him for three years and he divorced me as I had no children for him. Though other wives of his were there, yet he never appreciated my stay in his house without any child for him. After I went away, it was not long before I married my third husband who died during the first influenza attack. My fourth husband came while I was getting old, and he was a native of Oku Ibeku. All his wives had been killed by his enemies. I never wanted him in marriage at first, but when I heard of his sad news, I was in sympathy. Lastly, a bride-price was paid to my parents and off I went with my husband. When I went newly, I did not like the place because I noticed that the man did not get even one child. But I had to manage with him because he had many pieces of land for me to farm each year. This is the main reason I like staying here. My present husband is here with me but he had nothing doing because he does not see: he is blind and this has been the reason why he does not do any kind of work. Many of his wives died, so at the moment I am the only wife. I don't even think that anybody would like to marry him again. I like to marry him as long as I live so that I might have what to eat as he has got many farms.

I lived in my husbands' houses after leaving my parents. In those days girls were not permitted to stay away from their parents when they were not married. In the husband's house, women were not also at liberty to move about as the modern women do. A girl was considered to be good when she stayed indoors in her father's compound. For these reasons, I have never experienced life elsewhere than in my husbands' and parents' houses.

I like so much the place I am living because my husband has many lands which I can farm to earn a living. Even though all my former husbands died, yet I prefer my present husband to all others despite the fact that he does not see. With my present husband I consider life here to be the best because with farms I can afford to do anything I like and nobody struggles with me.

I was very small when I married my first husband. All my farms were planted to me by my mother even though they were not many as I was the smallest among all the wives. When I was a full-grown girl, I started farming as that was the only thing a married woman was expected to do by that time.

I had only one child for my first husband and since he died I never born any other child again.

I had a happy time when I married my very first husband newly. He neglected all other women and was highly interested in me. The love and happiness started to fade after I had delivered my first child who died. I enjoyed life when my mother-in-law was alive as she never gave the son a chance to cheat me. But since the woman died I had no other person to defend me and all my co-wives and even my husband considered me to be the worst woman he had ever married. Since I met with the hard luck in his house I never experienced happiness again as other women do.

It was not the custom of my people that a woman should marry more than one husband, but it was not within my power to keep the order because I was too small to have stayed without husband when my first and second husbands died.

The most interesting thing that happened to me was during the time I had my first pregnancy. I was too small to have been pregnanted. For that reason, people thought that I would not deliver the child in safety. But to their greatest surprise I delivered that child by God's power and without the help of any native midwife. When my mother-in-law who married me for her son heard of my safe delivery she was very happy and she bought many new dresses and utensils for me, to express her happiness. I considered that to be the most interesting thing that happened to me because in those days house utensils were often given to a girl by the girl's mother, but in my own case, I had it both from my mother and from my mother-in-law.

To me, I say that it is a good thing for a women whose husband has more than one wife because she will have other women to increase the husband's family. Any responsibility that should be on her shoulders alone would be shared according to the number of women that the man has. She will spend less money in feeding the husband because other wives are there to play their part as well. I say so because the majority of women in Ibibio, especially those in the rural areas, depend on farms given by the husbands. Therefore instead the husband gives his wife money for food, the wife will use the little she has in feeding the husband. In Ibibio land, when a man gives his wife one or two pieces of land to farm in a year, that wife is expected to maintain her own house as much as she could. In some homes women are always responsible in repairing their thatched houses, caring for the children both in sickness and otherwise, and seeing about all other responsibilities in the house. Judging from all these points, I say that it is a good thing for a woman whose husband marries more than one wife so that others might also help in carrying some of the husband's responsibilities that should be on one woman alone.

Nearly all members of my father's family are kind to me because I am the only daughter of my father who is now left.

The only good friend outside my family whom I have is my sister-in-law who is also married at this village. She likes seeing me every time and she always gives me useful advices. She cannot stay for a whole week without seeing me except she has no chance. She is always very helpful to me. Though she is not as old as myself, yet she has special interest for me and she always help me as much as she could. I have not helped her as she helps me but I usually visit her at my convenient time. She knows very well that I cannot have the strength to do some farm work for her because she is aware that I have many farms to work.

Well! I have enjoyed many more good changes than my mother did. In my mother's days, many of the things we are now having were not there. When Doctor Okpara came to Uyo, I was one of the selected women who joined motor to go and perform a traditional dance at Uyo in honour of Okpara. I have also joined another kind of engine boat to Greek Town where my mother never knew. Many new things I have seen these days were not there when my late mother was alive.

Even though most of these inventions and civilizations have brought war to some innocent people yet there are many that help to improve our respective villages and those that help in the rapid improvements of people. In days gone by, people lived with fears and superstition, but now anybody can travel anywhere provided the person has money. Before any death sentence is now passed on anybody all necessary investigations must be made to make sure that the person concerned is guilty of the offence. But in days gone by, there were no such things and some innocent people were killed or sold into slavery in any slightest offence committed.

Commentary

This story is chiefly interesting for the light it sheds on the disadvantages of child-marriage. The little girl in this case was too young even to sow the crops on the fields allotted to her, and she conceived a child at an age which caused concern for her life among the older women. After this she was twice widowed at an age when she could still be described as 'small'.

In the blind man's compound, all the cottages of his previous wives have fallen to dust, and his wife shares his house with no room of her own. This is an unconventional situation, but accounted for by the acute loneliness which the poor husband is said to feel when his wife is away at the farm.

She appears contented and is very hardworking, but her untidiness in dress is deplored by her neighbours, though they excuse it by saying that she has no children to teach her better.

A happily-married woman

I was born in a little village of Ikot Udo in Aba.

There was no birth registry at the time of my birth and coupled with that my parents were illiterate and had no record of my birth. I can guess I am now between fifty and fifty-five years of age.

I cannot estimate the date, but I was one of the last ones to be married of my age group. This was owing to many sicknesses. At one time my second cousin was sick too. When an oracle was consulted it was said that a relative of his mother should sacrifice before he should recover his health. I was selected to perform the sacrifice and he became well again. On this grounds, his mother decided to take me to him for a wife. Wonderful to say, the sickness which I frequently suffered no more attacked me. By that time I was about twenty-one years old.

I had married before, but as the first man was very poor and could not withstand my frequent sick complaints he took me back to my parents before one year of our marriage had passed. People advised him that as my heart had been taken away by wizards I would eventually die. Thereafter people never asked my hand in marriage except my present husband, who is still living.

He is at the moment a petty produce buyer, but formerly he was a teacher under the Church of Scotland Mission.

I am the only wife of my husband, and I have no co-wives.

During the early days of our marriage, when my husband was a teacher, I used to tour round with him to which ever station he was assigned. Since his resignation many years ago we had been staying here in Ikot Udo Aba. I had only one occasion of travelling to Enugu, the capital of Eastern Nigeria, when my daughter was in the Women's Training Centre.

I like best to stay in this village. I have been staying here most of my days and I love this pretty home of mine. I do not think my husband could have been able to train all my children if we were living elsewhere. Here we are very thrifty and we save some of the money we realize from our petty trade and our hand-press for production of palm oil. We engage in a little farming and the proceeds are what we feed on and in fact we use to sell out some of our product.

I can describe my life as a happy one. Even though we sometimes suffered the envy of some of our villagers, yet we live a contented life. We are sometimes hard up financially because of our children's school fees; but as my husband is liberal we use to get some friends come to our aid. I appreciate my husband's difficulties and I am never suspicious of his relationship with other women.

I look after my little farm and I do assist my husband in his trade. As for the palm press, I am solely responsible for its running.

I have seven children (five sons and two daughters) and six grandchildren.

I am always happy and the happiest time in my life was during the early days of our marriage. As I am related to my husband, he regards me as his sister and I regard him as my brother. He became much attached to me as it was through my hands that he was healed. I too became healed automatically as I entered his house. What is more when I feel that our marriage was ordained from above, I use to be very grateful to our God. Besides, he has blessed me with seven children, two of whom are presently studying overseas.

I have no idea of what you call unhappiness. Of course, I would reflect my mind to my youthful days when I was always sickly and without a husband. I may say that was my unhappiest moment in life.

I cannot imagine what it would feel like if I were married to a polygamist; but from the experience I have acquired from other women, I can say that marriage to a polygamist does not favour happiness and harmonious principles which any marriage should have. The women themselves have to admit a 'care less' attitude over any enviable condition in the family. Love charms which are said to influence the love a husband owes to his wife are very rampant in a polygamous family. Cases are reported where in an attempt to concentrate the husband's love on one woman, the husbands are poisoned to death or they become insane. I feel it regrettable for a woman when her husband marries more than one wife.

Certainly, among all people I know, my husband has been the

kindest to me and I have realized that I would be doing my family greater harm than good if I were to have a friend outside my family to whom I should confide. Nevertheless, we have casual friends: one of them was so kind to us that when we had financial difficulties in paying the school fees of our children, he assisted us by giving us a loan. Previously, my husband sponsored this man's education in the man's primary school years. He was one of our servants.

People say that I do resemble my mother in all ways. I do not think this statement is false nor does it exclude my manners.

Certainly, life has got better since the days when I was young.

Commentary

This woman is of a later generation than most of the others. Her husband has profited by education, and her children may be considered to belong to the new élite class. Although she has been to the capital, she is conscious of the attractiveness of her thatched cottage with its neat and well-polished furnishings. The average expatriate would certainly agree with her, but the usual African preference is for the cement blocked tin-roofed town house.

It is interesting that the close kinship between the husband and wife is seen as an additional factor in promoting domestic harmony.

She is bright, buxom, and fair-skinned, and wears the head-tie and shoes of a townswoman. She is said to be something of a 'hector' in behaviour.

The slave's daughter

I was born in one of the poorest families in Use Offot, a daughter to one of the slaves who was sold to the late chief of this village. Though my father was a slave yet due to his good behaviour, the chief who bought him according to the news was a little bit sympathetic with my father. Many attempts were made at killing my father but the chief did not give any consent to that, rather he adopted my father and later married a wife for him from outside the village. Slaves were often maltreated but in case of my father, it was not so because my father was a quiet and harmless man.

I married while I was about sixteen years of age because I spent most of my early life with the Methodist medical missionaries.

I should say I married once since I was born but I was pregnanted while I was still serving the missionaries. I was later given in marriage to my late husband as the man who pregnanted me never promised to marry me. My husband was asked to pay a certain sum of money which enabled him to adopt my first daughter with whom this different man pregnanted me.

My husband died on January 15th, 1967. He was humble and harmless, and was a friend of little children. He depended mainly on palm fruit cutting, palm wine tapping and petty native farming. Though he had not much money from these things, yet when I put him to light of the glories that one could rightly own in the education of one's children, for this reason, certain needs of life including the wearing of apparels and the eating of delicious foods were regarded by him as luxury. Rather, he tied a single loin cloth and went about his humble jobs of palm wine tapping, and so on. He later decided putting away earthly things and still to struggle for the education of his children.

When my co-wives married my husband newly, they pretended to be kind to me but within a short time, they stopped entirely because

166

they thought as a senior wife I was the one controlling my husband. They were also respectful at first but within a short time, they started showing their colours as those who considered themselves too big to respect their senior. Jealousy was the order of the day since they came into the family but my husband had never given them room to make it a habit.

I was his first wife but he later married the other wives who were not able to stay due to their jealousy and hatred and as they started creating trouble with my children.

I started life with the Methodist women missionaries. These missionaries were so much interested in me because they were made to understand how my father came to settle at Use as a slave to the late chief of that place. These missionaries were the people who helped to abolish slave-dealing in the areas. The missionaries also presented many gifts to the chief for having treated my father as his own son instead of killing him as others did.

When I left these missionaries to marry my late husband I did not at first enjoy this village because life in the village was very strange to me. But when I stayed for some time, I started enjoying the village. Though my husband had no fear of God in him when we married newly, I later convinced him to put away earthly things and enter the service of Jesus Christ under the Methodist Mission. Our house became a full Christian home and I like staying here more than any other place.

From my youth my life was a happy one according to how I was brought up. Here in the family, I became even happier because when I stepped into the home, my husband knew very little about God. I showed him the help that God could do for him, and he saw with me without hesitation. Through my assistance he ignored all luxuries and decided to train his children, so that we at last, saw the good fruits of his hard work, we felt so proud about it that he started to assume certain nicknames like 'A costly Gentleman' and 'The Poor with the Iron Heart' and 'The Unique Individual'.

Since I started life in my late husband's house, I did no other thing than farming because he was very rich in farm lands.

As for children, I have two males and three females.

My happiest time started when my two sons started life very progressively as a result of our hard labour. Another happiest moment was when these two sons built a magnificent building for us to live in. It was through this good example that my sons set, that made the inhabitants of this village as a whole, to devote their interest towards the training of both their sons and daughters.

My husband's death made me to be very unhappy because even though he was old, but yet he was still strong. People killed him because of hatred so that he might not stay longer to enjoy the fruit of his labour. Though he died while he was not so old, yet for all his sufferings, it was consoling to note that before he died, he has had the benefit of owning changes of clothing besides living and dying in a pan-roofed house.

The most interesting thing that happened to me was during the time that my first son was promoted as a senior Nursing Superintendent in Wesley Guild Hospital, Illeshia in Western Nigeria. Though he was not well trained when he joined the nursing work, but through his intelligence, he was able to achieve success as a result of his hard work and sincerity in the job.

To the best of my knowledge, I say it is always a bad thing for a woman when the husband has more than one wife. There has never been any peace in a polygamous family. In days gone by, men who married many wives were often regarded as the most richest men. Women whose husbands married many wives often enjoyed the married home because they were not so much after luxuries as the modern women. They depended wholly and entirely on their farms, while the modern women are depending on their husbands. These are some of the reasons that many wives find it difficult to make a happy home in a polygamous family.

I have no friend outside my family. My children are the people who are now kindest to me. They do everything within their power to make me forget about my late brothers, sisters and relatives, who passed away during the last influenza attack.

I don't confide with anybody else other than my children. And they have satisfied me more than others could do. If any of them comes from his or her station, I usually cook for them. I also help in nursing their children as well as their mother would do. Immediately their children are up to one year, I always asked the parents to send them to me so that the children might be familiar with me.

My life is different from that of my parents in dressing, the way of behaving, eating delicious foods, and knowing what is good and that which is bad. Things moved very slow and backward but now civilization makes things very simple and plain.

Commentary

A lifetime of Christianity and the consciousness of virtue rewarded have nevertheless not persuaded this widow of the possibility of death from natural causes. She has been a powerful person in her time, and appears to have disposed of her junior co-wives without difficulty.

Although living in what her neighbours consider to be a magnificent house, and eating 'delicious' food, she remains inconsolable. Her children visit her continually to comfort her.

A travelled woman

I was born in one of the largest families here in Ibiaku Uruan. As I was first daughter to a well-to-do man, one of his richest friends in Eman Uruan married me after my father had refused many men to marry me in my village. I have not been married more than once. I was widowed when I was too old to marry a second husband.

I was about fifteen years of age when I married my late husband.

My husband died about four years ago. He was not all that old as he should die as early as that but, as an intelligent fellow, he was one of the court sitting members in the clan, he was loved by many who understood his good services not only in the village but in the clan as a whole. There were other wicked souls especially some of his brothers who considered all his good services as a kind of pride and these were the people who arranged and killed my innocent husband with their witchcraft. Even though he died, yet all his children are now enjoying the good work of their father.

My husband started life as a tailor. As the occupation could fetch him no reasonable income, he divided his time between farming and tailoring. He became one of the intelligent persons in the village and this fetched him an unqualified reputation. He was unanimously nominated to represent our area in all native authority administrations. He was the man to whom the Resident handed the key to the strong room of Uyo treasury. When the job was given to educated men, he was awarded a contract of constructing Uyo Ikpa road. He suggested having a uniform currency in our district as the then manillas and bracelets were still in use. He died the president of Uruan native court. Besides his various occupations he usually made up his living with his farm products.

I had over twenty co-wives and only six of the lot were left in the compound when he died. I would describe their feelings as being factious. With my last two co-wives I commanded some respectful attitude, I was very jealous of my first two co-wives and very envious of the love of my husband's fourth wife. Moreover, these feelings were very pronounced at some periods of the year namely, the sowing season and the mid-year harvest season.

But for a short time when I visited my son-in-law at Jos in Northern Nigeria, I have never lived outside my village. Of course my visit at Jos was not for pleasure trip but my son-in-law sent for me to come and attend the hospital at Jos. When I visited Jos it appears I was in a trance. I seemed to have gone to the land beyond this earth. I have seen the train and journeyed in it for the first time. Before I was admitted in the hospital, my son-in-law took me to the airport for the first time in my life. At the airport, I witnessed a plane taking off and another touching down. Of the people I met during the journey, I think that we here are between the extremes of life. I met some people who went quite neked* and others who dressed like the whites.

If it were possible for me to live and die in a township, I could have preferred the township to the village life. The language difficulty still withstanding I like to live in Jos. Living in fear is completely ruled out. The whiteman has turned nights to day in townships because of the electricity lights. One can move about till twelve o'clock midnight without any fear. I do not think witchcraft is practised anywhere except in villages. The security of one's life is not threatened by these foes. People eat a variety of food in townships and this is not common in villages. Old and young women in Jos considered dressing, but here we do not care about the type of dress we put on because everybody is busy working for their daily food. At Jos, I seem to have forgotten about some superstitious beliefs which constituted the fear of the villager.

It is rather difficult for me to say when I was happiest. My life in my husband's house was never a happy one as I had to contend with many difficulties in life. I have never experienced the love of a husband. No care was given to me during my months of pregnancy. I had to toil to maintain not only my children but also my husband. As my husband had no heart to attend any of us during sickness, I grieved not this deficiency rather his unconcerned attitude toward my sick children sickened my heart. Nevertheless as all my children are quite independent and there is not much to disturb my mind now, I am happier.

* As pronounced.

There are few occupations a woman can undertake which I have not undertaken.

(a) *Trading*: I started life as a trader and palm oil and kernels were my regular commodities. A tub of kernels or one cwt was sold at two manillas, that's 6*d*, or exchanged for a yard of cloth. One tin of palm oil cost 1*s* 6*d*. We had to convey these produce to Ifiayong beach—16 miles, or Nsai Market—10 miles. There was no standard value for these things, the better market was conducted at Nsai but the whites at Ifiayong beach used to pay cash for the commodities.

(b) *Production*: I use to splice rope for native fishing net. I would go to the woods and cut the plants called 'Ndidi'. The bark of this plant can be removed and scraped into yarns; and the yarns used for preparing native loin cloths. It entails a great task but as it was a source of income I did not count on the labour.

(c) *Farming*: Trading on these palm products is not conducive to my old age. I am doing just a little of the rope splicing and farming is now my main occupation. Of course, this is only to maintain my life.

I now have four children, twenty grandchildren, and three great-grandchildren.

The happiest time in my life cannot be given as I am still living so I may experience happier moments in the future. Nevertheless, I was very happy when I returned from Jos where I was admitted into the hospital. I came back very rich financially and physically. I had many gifts and also my health was much improved. I also enjoyed an honour when my first daughter was married. As the first daughter in her family, much was paid on her behalf. The ceremonies which accompanied her marriage were very interesting. Presents poured in from the family of the husband and her father's; and being the first daughter of a village chief, my daughter was initiated into some cultural societies which women scarcely take part in. The glamour the ceremonies attained bestowed much pride on me the mother. These can be said to have been the happiest moments in my life.

The unhappiest moment in my life came when I lost my 'angel' daughter through the plague called 'Effiom Nsa'—influenza. The epidemic caught three of my children simultaneously. There were no qualified doctors nor was the remedy known. People died in scores. I had to convey them to a prayer house and that was the time the spiritual church was nearly introduced to our community. I had none but my poor mother to assist me.

During the year when influenza ravaged the whole community

there were many death cases. But one thing common with us is that, we think nobody has ever died a natural death; nor could we reasonably accept the plague without associating it with wicked hands of wizards. This being the case, a group of persons were suspected as having infected the atmosphere with some poisonous gas which they purchased purposely to cause the havoc. At that time, there were no judicial courts; rather the suspected had to defend themselves by swearing at a juju shrine or eating the calabar beans. Held by this bias, I rejoiced that the man responsible for the death of my child would eventually die. On an appointed day, these people were summoned to a special tribunal which tried them. They were all caused to chew calabar beans. The beans, it was said, would poison the blood of anyone who was guilty and the innocent would go free. To be very candid, the two species of the beans are quite poisonous and any person who chewed them died within a short while. This notwithstanding they were forced to eat the fruit and within a short while they all died away, not because they were perhaps at fault but that the village had wanted to get rid of these men whom they suspected without any proof.

In those days a woman had to depend on what she can produce from her farms, and when a man's riches were exaggeratedly associated with the number of wives he married, to be a member of a polygamous family was applauded with some pride. Then education was yet to be given a place in the economy of our society. Children born were made to follow the natural occupations which existed then—they had to be fishermen or farmers and nothing more. But now things have changed and men do not have to live by the soil alone. With my recent experiences I have come to the judgment that it is a bad thing for both a woman and her children when her husband marries more than one wife. A few years ago we had cases in which the more beloved wives persuaded the husband not to educate children from the other wives. The effect was quite a bitter one not only to the child but also to the family at large.

I was very unfortunate to belong to a group of these nominal wives. We of the group loved each other a bit and showed a little kindness to one another. In this group strife could hardly be ruled out and I cannot say anyone was kind to me except my children who were the lot I had in this world.

I did have a woman friend with whom I used to share the purchase of palm fruits. Along with, during the cultivating period of the year, we used to give ourselves* mutual assistance at work. Though we sometimes helped ourselves* financially, yet her frequent and more significant help was in settling quarrels between my husband and me.

Until I became quite old, I used to help her in conveying her palm oil and kernels to Ifiayong beach. Besides, we strengthen the bond of our friendship by constant invitation of one another to a love meal. There have never been a substantial financial help I ever rendered to her.

If my mother were to wake from the grave today, she would look on this village and the dwellers as being a race from the heavens. She died while I was quite a kid. During their days people knew no clothes, people up to the age of fifteen wore nothing at all. Only people who were considered adults, who had gone out of the fattening room, were qualified to wear a little piece of cloth like material around their waist. The cloth 'ikipya' was made of rafia. The body besides the waist was left neked. Even when clothes were available in the community, some did not like putting it on. The headkerchiefs were not tied in the way you see them, rather women carried them on their heads folded. Today women rub sweet smelling oil to smoothen their bodies, but my mother rubbed ordinary cooking oil. Other ornamentals included two types of native chalk and sap from a tree. The red chalk was rubbed around the sole of the feet, the palms and sometimes on the face. The white chalk which was more washable than the red was used mainly decorating the whole body. The third was used occasionally especially when one village was invited by another for a dance display. As this was black and the stain very lasting, not many people like to use it. When we were young a single motor cycle passing would attract the whole lot of people; we children would lie on the track to smell the odour of the petrol. Buildings were well constructed, but my mother had never seen a cemented wall house with pan roof.

Indeed, I feel life has got better with me since my children can assist me. I feel quite happy when my grandchildren come to me.

Commentary

A particularly admirable specimen of African womanhood, this lady, though totally uneducated and retaining many traditional superstitions, shows originality, detachment and criticism. Despite receiving

* Each other.

neither love nor consideration from her husband, her loyalty to him is boundless. She has had no real opportunity to become a 'woman of two worlds' but has nevertheless an intuitive grasp of the alternative systems of ethics existing in colonial Africa.

She has made some attempt at furnishing her cottage, and has hung the walls with old pictures.

The witch's great-grand-daughter

I was born at Mbiabong, one of the smallest villages of Etoi Clan. I am one of the great-granddaughters of a certain wicked woman who was one of the best witches of that village.

Though there was no birth record kept, yet I can estimate my age according to the number of years that one Okon Ibanga brought the first Spiritual Church to this village. Some elderly men in my family told me that it was that year I was born. And they also told me that it was that year which all the old women witches were revealed by one of the best prophets of that Spiritual Church.

Due to this wicked woman who practised witchcraft, I understood that when I was two and a half years old, my parents took me to this Spiritual Church, handed me over to this Prophet in charge of the Spiritual Church, and asked him to adopt me as one of his daughters so that I might no longer be harmed by the wicked old woman who practised witchcraft. I grew to be a full-grown person in the house of my adopted father, who put me in the fattening room and later handed me over to one of his sons for marriage. My real parents never received anything on behalf of me as a bride-price because they were very happy to see how my adopted father maintained me in good faith as if I was his real daughter.

My husband died many years ago. But before he died, he warned me not to go out of his compound nor to marry any other man after his death. He told me that as long as I remained in his name, even though he was dead, he will still be in a position to protect me and my children. I was contented with what he said and after these sayings he spat in front of me and confirmed his speeches before he died.

During his life time, he joined his father to work with him in the Spiritual Church. And with that he was able to achieve the same mystic power as the father himself; he released so many men and women who were tortured by the strong organized groups of witches.

I was his first wife. Others who were married later on died before my husband himself was dead. They were respectful to me as a senior wife of their husband. All of us were considerate to each other and when they died I was the one taking good care of the children, till all of them grew up. Nobody jealoused each other because we were contented with anything our husband was able to give us. Nobody was cheated as everything including lands for farming were shared to us according to the order of greatness.

I have not lived elsewhere since I was born because even before my husband died he warned me not to move out of his compound and I still maintain that till this present time.

I have already said that I have not experienced anywhere else in life than where I am now living. I do not know whether I should have liked some other place in life more than this place, if I had the chance of experiencing elsewhere. But at the moment I like this village more than any other place because it is the village where I was born.

My life is indeed a happy one because I was able to maintain what my late husband said and that also contributed to my progress and that of my four children as a whole. As far as this family is concerned, I am respected as well as my children. Even though my husband was dead, yet there is no discrimination between other members of the family and my own children. Things are still moving fine with me in the family.

I have four children, with ten grandchildren and one great-grand-son.

I have been doing petty farming and petty trading for most of my years.

The happiest time in my life was the time my husband died. It does not mean that I was happy for his death, but I was happy because he told me many encouraging words before he parted from me. That really proved his sincerity of love towards me.

The most unhappiest time for me was the time my real mother died. My mother was killed after she had given birth to twin daughters. It was a very strong law in those days that no woman must born twins in the village. And it was believed that when a woman delivered twins in a village, all juju powers of such village must no longer be active, so that a very strong law was passed on whosoever will bring such a sinful act to quench the power of the juju. My mother was disgraced in one of the oldest twin markets of this village and later she was taken to the forest named 'Akai Mbubiat', or 'The unclean Forest', and there they tied my mother with rope on one of the cotton trees, there she suffered until lastly she died. When this thing happened to my mother, I had a very sad time for almost three years. Even though it was the custom that twin mothers were to be punished so, yet I was so much disturbed in mind as such a thing occurred to my mother, who had suffered alone in the house after having handed me to a man who adopted me provided my life was secured.

The thing that interests me much in my life was when my great-grandmother, who was very active in the act of witchcraft died. During her life time, she disturbed children much in the family and it was herself who caused my brothers and sisters death. When she died, her head was cut off to an active native doctor who bought the head and placed it in front of his shrine so that it might no longer come back through devil spirit to destroy the family as she did during her life time. She was the only woman who caused a lot of destructions in my father's family and since she died there was peace in the family.

When a woman has many co-wives, she will not be so much worried about her husband if even she is not in the house because she knows there are other co-wives to care for her husband. Her children will be cared for by other co-wives if she is away instead of leaving them alone in the house. The family of her husband will be increased by the help of other co-wives.

My father's brother is the person who is kindest to me. He is the only person in my father's family who usually visits me. During harvest, he usually gives me plenty yams from his farm.

I have no friend outside my family whom I can confide in. I have many friends in my husband's family to whom I confide. My husband's sister is one of them. She was very good to me during my days of pregnancy. She was the person who had been helping me in my farm work any time I delivered a child. When I was out from the fattening room she bought many clothes for me and my new born baby. When one of my children grew up, I sent the child to go and stay with her because she had nobody to help in the house. That child stayed with her until the child was up to the age of marriage.

I am living a clean and plain life while my mother was living under superstition and fear. I experienced many more things than my mother did. During my mother's days, there was no main road, no bicycle, nor motor, no good markets; schools were not there nor any of them knew the value of training one's children; rather they employed their children as fishermen so that they might have plenty fish to eat. In my mother's days they believed in what I should say 'Do me I do you' or 'tid for tad', but these days things like that are not existing.

Life has got better than the days I was young. In those days I still remembered when the Methodist missionaries came to open a hospital in our village, but my village heads thought that if they give the missionaries land to build the hospital, in future they would no longer have surplus lands to plant their crops. They did that because they did not consider the missionaries as good people as themselves, especially when they saw the difference in their skin. This days things are not like that again. We have expatriates mixing up with the Africans and they are the people who have brought in more light into our interior villages. Killing of twins and their mothers are no longer in existence. Fear and superstitious beliefs have been ruled out.

Commentary

The father-in-law in this story would appear to be an adept in bride-price avoidance. It would be interesting to know how many daughters in-law he recruited in this fashion. His 'Spiritual Church' must not be confused with a mission. It was apparently successful, as his son was the first person in his village to build a permanent house. The story-teller occupies three rooms in this building, as senior wife.

She has an excellant reputation in her village for supporting other women who are in need, in consequence of which she never requires to hire labourers for help in her farm, as her women friends always repay her kindness with assistance in the fields.

She is modern in appearance, and youthful-looking on account of tinting her hair—an unusual practice in a countrywoman. She is also the village representative of the Etoi women's association.

A lady member of Ekpo

I was born in Ikot Oku Nsit in Uyo Division, in one of the oldest families of Usuk Uma Adiaha. (Adiaha means first-born daughter. This signifies that in Nigeria, until lately, children were yet answering names for their mothers.)

My age is highly impossible for me to know because in those days nobody valued birth records nor did our early parents regard it to be of any significance. When I grew up, my late mother showed me a certain woman who was born the same day as I was. This was the only method by which children's birth records were maintained in my village that time. With this nobody can know a particular time or month in a year that his or her child was born as the modern men and women do. Besides, as one farming area was cleared once in seven years' time, children's ages were every seven years accounted.

I married during the time I was wearing only one and a half yards of cloth. My parents gave me to go and stay with the senior wife of my husband whom I served for many years before the husband came out to marry me as a second wife. In those days, men prized girls with good manners as high as men this days regards working-class ladies* for marriage. During my stay in my mistress's house, her husband was highly interested in me because I was very smart and industrious in the house. These were the reason that my master came out and paid for my bride-price while I was even very small. After the bride-price had been paid, I continued to live with my husband's senior wife until I was up graded to a real house wife.

I have married only once since I was born. In those days, it was the custom in my father's family that, when any girl was married out of the family, she must not divorce the husband whether for good or for bad. It was believed that when a girl divorces the husband, the

* Employed city girls (clerks, shop assistants, etc.).

parents of the girl would be regarded as those who never gave their daughters good home training.

My husband died many years ago. My senior son is the person who maintains me up to the present time. If I had not got him, life would have been very bad with me. When my husband died, my senior son was small and I was asked to choose any man I love to marry in the family, but I refused because I was a senior person to all those men whom I was asked to choose for marriage. Even though I suffered as a widow, yet all the bitterness turned to happiness, good health and long life when my son became a full-grown man. My son was not educated but I spent the little I had to train him on how to carve a canoe and with that he was able to build a house of his own, marry a wife, feed me and his entire family.

My son, as I have already said, is a carpenter and he is one of the experts in canoe making. As far as I know, he can make a mighty canoe which can be used in sailing to Fernando-Po and other foreign lands without any complain. Through his good work, he was once awarded a carved knife by one of the early Portuguese who were at that time buying palm produce with the people of Ifiayong, or Usiak Ifia as it was then called.

As my late husband was a chief native doctor in the whole of this village, he married many wives. In those days a man was highly respected according to the number of wives he could marry. Though bride-price was not as high as it is these days, yet it was not a simple thing to marry a wife because men never had many sources of earning money as I see the present men do. In my husband's case, many of his wives were given to him free of charge so that my husband might protect their lives. Some of these girls were born in wicked and destructive families and their parents thought that the best they could do to save their lives was to give them free of charge to active native doctors like my husband so that he could protect their lives whenever their enemies came to attack them. My husband married thirteen wives out of his money but eight other wives were given to him free of charge provided their lives were secured. (Twenty-one wives on the whole.)

As I was not his first, second, nor third wife, I was not all that respected. Women were many and any sensible woman did not bother herself about that, some of the old women were anyhow more respected as I was then a small girl and newly married. The older wives were kind to me at first but later they thought it was a cheat for them to be kind to a newly-married girl who could not afford to return their kindness. Jealousy was always the order of the day especially during the farming season as we are now in it. Some of my co-wives often accused my husband of failing to give them a better farm, that is a more fertile. Cases like that created much jealousy among us; and with this many of us usually stayed many months without saying hello! to one another. During these periods my late husband usually suffered because those wives who feel that my husband has cheated them will overlook my husband and all services will have a breakdown until my husband must call outsiders to come in for settlement. During that time, the unhappy wives will not mind whether my husband eats or not, but all they know is to cook their food and eat with their children so that my husband might repent when it gets to such season the following year.

I lived then in my husband's compound, but when my son grew up he bought a land and a house of his own where I am now living in peace and without any trouble.

I like rather to live in my son's compound than going back to either my husband's compound or anywhere else. My daughters-in-law are respectful to me as well as my grandchildren. Nobody is jealous of me or disregards me as it was in my husband's compound.

My life is indeed a happy one even though I have only one son at the moment yet he has done all he could for me as a mother who struggled for his future progress.

Farming was my occupation, but since I became very sick I have not been able to do that again. In those days, farm crops were not as costly as I see these days, but it was very useful to us as all the food we needed came from the farm. In those days women never demanded any money from their husbands, as I see the modern women do. That was the reason why women in our days were even stronger than some of the men these days because they knew that if they did not work very hard they would not get what to eat. The modern women are very wasteful to their respective husbands because they do not know how to farm and their manners are very bad when comparing them with those women in my days. They are not only lazy, but they do not owe any respect to their respective husbands as we did during our days. In those days, girls were married once and for all but now a girl of fifteen or seventeen years of age can experience life with two or three thusbands in a space of four or five years. They do not also keep themselves only to their husbands so that they might meet their wants with which perhaps their husbands cannot equip them satisfactorily. In those days, married women often died during their pregnancy if they made the mistake of meeting with other men. These days such traditions have died natural deaths and women have become very rough and insincere to their husbands.

I had two male and one female children, but two died leaving only my first son who marries three wives with eleven children.

The happiest time in my life started when my son built a house of his own. His father's sons cheated him so much while we were staying altogether, because they knew my son had no brother or sister to defend him. But since he built his house, nobody has been disturbing him again.

The most unhappy moment in my life was the time my only daughter died while in the fattening room after three days' fever.

The most interesting thing that happened to me was when my son became both a full member of both the 'Ekpo and the Ekpe' societies. That day I was well dressed in a traditional way. While my son entertained the men, I was busy entertaining the women who later appointed me the first woman of the village to be a woman member in 'Ekpo' society. Since that year, I knew all the secrets about 'Ekpo' and how it can be arranged, but it was a confidential matter except to all women and men who are members.

Life is better with a woman who has many co-wives than the one who has not. The woman whose husband has more than one wife will have other co-wives to help in feeding the husband. If the wives were three in number, they would arrange for the husband's meals among three of them, so that it may not bother one wife alone. If one wife is not fortunate enough to deliver children, the husband will not so much bother her because other fortunate wives are there to born children for him. If a woman whose husband marries her alone quarrels with the husband, it will be difficult for two of them to reconcile, but if there are other co-wives, they can easily settle the case between their husband and the co-wife. A woman whose husband has more than one wife will not feel lonesome if the husband travels out of the village or to the seaside, because she will have other co-wives to stay happily in the compound until the husband returns.

Everybody in my parents' family is all dead except me. The grandchildren do not regard me as their own and I do not confide my hope on them even though I do not have many children.

I had friends while I was not as old as I am, but since all my age groups died, I do not have interest in things like that any longer.

My life is almost the same with that of my mother despite all changes and higher development of life. I find it difficult to adopt the modern way of living because I was brought up under primitive societies.

To me, I would still like people to live the type of life that we had before. In those days people ruled peacefully and there was no disturbances as we are now having. In those days, law breakers were often sold into slavery but now such people are guaranteed to do worst by prisoning them; there they are well fed and well cared for so that when they are set free, they come and do the worst so that they might again be taken to a place where they will stay free and save their money and food in the house. I so much prefer the old method we lived in olden days to the present way of living which is full of blood-shed, evil practices and hatred. Since we handed over our country to be ruled by those who considered themselves to know more than our forefathers did, there is no more peace to poor people. People are forced to pay heavy taxes whereas in days gone by, these set of people never paid taxes. Those are the reasons why I say that life has got worst these days than the days I was young.

Commentary

Certainly the oldest in appearance of the old ladies in this book, she is quite toothless, and dirty enough to excite the disgust of her neighbours, one of whom complained that her finger-nails were black as those of a monkey, her grandchildren refusing to eat with her for the same reason. Nevertheless, they are unanimous in praising her excellent complexion. She is indifferent to matters of dress, and eats little, spending what money her son gives her on tobacco.

She is however a highly sociable old person, ready to welcome any visitor, and she is much in demand on moonlight nights by the children, who gather round her special chair to listen to her stories.

A nursing sister

My village is one of the small villages in Etoi clan in Uyo Province.

I am about fifty-four years of age. Though there was no record kept about my birth date, yet my mother told me that she conceived my about seven months before the people of Efiat came to perform 'Nyori' dance in my village. I asked my father, who was a village head, and having counted the number of times they have planted on a particular farm, I calculated my age to be what I have mentioned above.

I married when I was about twenty-seven years of age. The marriage lasted for only six months and I again became an unmarried lady for seven years. It was a terrible incident in the history of the Etoi clan.

The man who is marrying me at the moment is my second husband and he is a brother to my late husband. I got married at the age of twenty-seven as I had already said. After three years of courtship, we agreed to marry. A bride-price has to be paid. As both of us were Roman Catholic members, we had to wed in the church immediately as I was under three months pregnancy. If not that I was conceived immediately we married, perhaps I should have been married to my husband at least six months before the great incident occurred. But I can be frank to say that I did not enjoy the marriage before death came in and put a strong barrier between the two of us. The day was fixed for the wedding and all necessary arrangements made to prove all that was done secretly before the people. Attending the service were over two thousand people including nearly all the nurses in the hospital where I was working. Teachers and schoolchildren from the school where my late husband was teaching. Reverend sisters and nurses from other catholic Missions were countless. It was indeed a happy and glorious day for two of us, but see how the happiness was badly spoiled in the middle of the day, after the marriage had been blessed in the church. After church blessing, everybody had to go down to my husband's village, which is about two miles from the church, for entertainment. The bride and the bridegroom had to be taken down first with a procession of nurses who were around me. When it was about ten poles to the compound the car had an accident and my husband died on the spot. All the nurses were seriously wounded and died one after the other at the dispensary and maternity situated around the junction where the accident occurred. It was indeed a piteous day for the people of Etoi as a whole. And that was how I missed my husband. According to the regulation of the Church, I was not permitted to marry anybody else until after seven years. After I had completed the seven years, circulars were sent to nearly all the Roman Catholic churches in Eastern Nigeria, as called by then, before an authority was given for me to choose anybody I like for marriage. My husband's junior brother was chosen and I have got two children for him.

Fortunately, my present husband is still living and I so much pray for his long life for I have really suffered in marriage affairs. He is a teacher and he has had experience in the job for fifteen years now. I have no co-wife for the Church to which we belong does not permit that. We married in the Christian way and we still hope to maintain this honour and prestige until our last day.

Since I grew up to know myself, I spent most of my life at Ifiayong Girls' School, where I passed my standard six as it was then called. After my school days I spent most of my life at St Luke's Hospital, Anua, where I was employed as a nurse. And this is where I stay since I started my job until the present time.

I like to stay where I am at the moment because it is the place that I am stationed. My late husband built a house in this place which means that I will never go away from Anua even if I am retired. Secondly, Anua is a semi-township and I have been accustomed to staying in an open place like Anua. My husband is also stationed here.

My life is indeed a happy one because my mother has been telling me how they were suffering in days gone by. She told me that in her days there was nothing like the blessing of marriage because nearly all men married many wives. People always married according to native law and custom. Woman valued men with many lands for farming more than the working-class men. This happened because they thought a woman could not have sufficient food to eat where there was no sufficient lands to farm on. I can witness that the modern women prefer working-class men to those who depend wholly and entirely on their farms. I enjoy the happiness of marriage more than my mother because I don't share my husband with any co-wife as my mother did. I can dress in more decent and attractive way than my mother did. With money I can travel to anywhere on pleasure trip with my husband without any fear. I am civilized and this has helped to bring in happiness as required in life.

I started my life as a nurse and that is still my job. In those days, those who had their standard six certificates were requested to work in any branch they preferred. With my little qualification I joined the job but now I am one of the sister-nurses in this field.

I have three sons and a daughter. All of them have finished their elementary schools. My daughter has been given in marriage but she has no child yet. My elder son is now overseas studying medicine under the sponsorship of our Mission. Two younger ones are in secondary schools. I have no grandchildren yet. I am expecting that very soon from my daughter.

The happiest time in my life was the time our Mission authorized me to choose another husband in place of my deceased one.

The unhappiest time in my life was the time I missed my former husband by death in the most disgraceful way.

The most interesting thing that happened to me was the time I was qualified as a registered sister-nurse as for this I had all the time been praying to achieve in life.

In my opinion as a Christian, I say that it is a bad thing for a woman when the husband has more than one wife; with reasons. Her children will not be properly cared for. The wife will not gain special interest from the husband as she ought to. She will not be bold to present any of her secrets before the husband in case the husband disclosed the same to others whom perhaps he loved more than the other one. The wife gains less love from the husband because she is not the only wife of the husband. She can stay for two or three years without even an earring from the husband because the so-called husband has thousands of commitments around him. She will only answer housewife but does not see any difference in her as a housewife in the real sense of it.

The only person of my parents' family who is kindest to me is my senior brother. The rest pretend to love me, but they are not inwardly interested in my affairs.

I have many people outside my family in whom I can confide. All of them are my co-workers and two of them are expatriates working also in the Mission.

They helped me in any way they can especially in giving me pieces of advice. They have never helped me financially because I have never presented such requests before them. I also show them my kindness as a good friend.

I am educated but my mother is not. I am civilized but my mother is not because in her days there was no civilization. If I am sick today, I will approach a doctor for immediate treatments but my mother does not so much believe in medical treatment rather in herbs because it is the way she was brought up. I know different kinds of diets I can take to keep me younger but my mother does not believe on such things as she feels most of the diets are only made for white people. I can dress in a more decent and attractive way than my mother can do.

Life has got better since the days I was young. Every day we get many good changes in life than before. These changes have also helped to improve the general standard of living than before. People are well qualified to suit with the different changes we have in the present-day world.

Index

Index

For Product Safety Concerns and Information please contact our EU
representative GPSR@taylorandfrancis.com
Taylor & Francis Verlag GmbH, Kaufingerstraße 24, 80331 München, Germany

www.ingramcontent.com/pod-product-compliance
Lightning Source LLC
Chambersburg PA
CBHW070428270326
41926CB00014B/2983